HIRING SMART

HIRING SMART
How to Hire a Team That Wants to Work

THOMAS J. WINNINGER

PRIMA PUBLISHING

© 1997 by Thomas J. Winninger

All rights reserved. No part of this book may be reproduced or transmitted in any form or by any means, electronic or mechanical, including photocopying, recording, or by any information storage or retrieval system, without written permission from Prima Publishing, except for the inclusion of quotations in a review.

PRIMA PUBLISHING and colophon are registered trademarks of Prima Communications, Inc.

Library of Congress Cataloging-in-Publication Data

Winninger, Thomas J.
   Hiring smart : how to hire a team that wants to work / by Thomas J. Winninger.
     p.   cm.
   Includes index.
  ISBN 0-7615-0618-7
   1. Employees — Recruiting. 2. Employee selection. I. Title.
HF5549.5.R44W497   1996
658.3'11—dc20   96-19412
                                                                                     CIP
96 97 98 99 AA 10 9 8 7 6 5 4 3 2 1
Printed in the United States of America

How to Order:
Single copies may be ordered from Prima Publishing, P.O. Box 1260BK, Rocklin, CA 95677; telephone (916) 632-4400. Quantity discounts are also available. On your letterhead, include information concerning the intended use of the books and the number of books you wish to purchase.

Contents

Acknowledgments   vii
Introduction   ix

Chapter 1: Puzzle Wrapped in a Riddle: How to Find Quality Employees   1

Chapter 2: Strategies and Ideas   9

Chapter 3: Secret Hiring Bait of Small Businesses: Job Satisfaction   19

Chapter 4: Recruiting: A Job for You   31

Chapter 5: Employees As Recruiters   35

Chapter 6: Hire Your Own Employees Before Someone Else Does   41

Chapter 7: New Ways to Use Employment Agencies   51

Chapter 8: How to Hire Women: Reduce Stress in Their Lives   55

Chapter 9: My Customer, My Employee   63

Chapter 10: Become a Light in the Night   67

Chapter 11: The School Connection   75

**Chapter 12: Indirect Recruiting:
   Offer Education**   81

Chapter 13: Play Your Network   87

**Chapter 14: Flex Your Schedule
   to Lure Employees**   91

Chapter 15: Brochures for the VCR   103

**Chapter 16: Advertising Alternative:
   Marketing**   111

**Chapter 17: Creativity with Targeted
   Mailing Lists**   119

**Chapter 18: An Ounce of Retention Is
   Worth a Pound of Recruitment**   125

**Chapter 19: Retention Tip:
   Hire the Already Motivated**   135

Chapter 20: Retaining Through Training   145

**Chapter 21: Employment Screening
   for Your Company**   155

Index   165

ACKNOWLEDGMENTS

My appreciation to Steve Franzmeier for his help in making this book a reality. I am grateful to Wendy Zhorne, whose strong belief in the project became absolutely contagious. Finally, thank you to great examples of team developers: Jim Lind, Amoco; Fred Whyte, Stihl Chain Saw; Dick Young, Behler Young; Tom Pall, Southwestern Bell Yellow Pages; and Ray Kroc, McDonalds.

INTRODUCTION

How can I find good, qualified people to work for me? And once I've hired them, how do I elicit their best possible performance?"

That's the topic that I am most often asked to address in the hundred or so speeches that I deliver each year to small, independent business groups. The concerns are always the same:

- "Crowds of applicants used to respond to my 'Help Wanted' ads. But not anymore."
- "It's difficult to find job applicants who have even the *basic* skills."
- "I can't compete with salaries offered by the big company down the street."
- "Self-motivated employees are as rare as passenger pigeons."

Great distress prevails among independent businesspeople in most parts of America today. They are troubled because the growth and, sometimes, the very survival of their organizations are threatened by a shortage of qualified, motivated employees.

To the disgusted and the desperate, I say: Be of good cheer. Abandon your want ads, your nepotism, your employment agencies, and your government job-finding services. Follow me; I will show you where the good people are and how to reach them.

Apply the ideas in this book and you, too, shall be all smiles. You will have trustworthy, enthusiastic, creative, and responsible people filling your jobs. This book shows readers how to develop a human-resource pool that ensures long-term business success, reduces turnover, and improves the quality and the skills of entry-level people.

These results are achieved by taking action in four strategic areas:

1. Finding solutions to problems.
2. Using uncommon sources to locate talented and motivated people.
3. Employing techniques that show how to tap the uncommon sources effectively and inexpensively.
4. Designing a plan of action that develops a continuous flow of applicants in less than thirty-six months.

This book outlines ways to find "suspects" (seemingly qualified people) who advance to the "prospect" stage after testing, interviews, and additional evaluation. (A "prospect" is a qualified candidate you'd like to hire.)

"[The need for qualified workers] is a nationwide business community problem, one that's especially acute for companies that require entry-level workers who are able to perform more tasks than those workers who join large firms," says Robert Martin, executive director of the Center for Work Force Preparation and Quality Education of the U.S. Chamber of Commerce.

In a survey of one thousand employers, almost seventy-five percent reported difficulty in finding qualified workers for reasons such as these:

- A labor force that is growing more slowly because there are fewer young people to enter the job market.
- Decline in the quality of U.S. education and a burgeoning skills deficit.

- Increasing mismatch between skills needed in the workplace and skills that workers possess.

In late 1991, the National Association of Manufacturers announced results of a survey of four hundred manufacturing companies in every part of the country. Results showed that companies turn away five of six applicants because they are unqualified.

- Two out of three companies said that most job applicants lack motivation and/or general skills needed to be productive.
- More than one-third of companies regularly turn down job applicants because they can't read or write well enough to hold a job.
- One-fourth of responding companies reported that they turn down applicants because of inadequate math and communication skills.

Of sixteen million workers entering the job market in the 1990s, only about twenty-five percent will possess the basic skills necessary to perform entry-level clerical or manufacturing work without remedial training, according to a 1991 article in *Personnel Journal*.

The Conference Board, a nonprofit business information organization, reports that nearly twenty percent of companies surveyed had trouble finding applicants who can read well enough to qualify for entry-level jobs.

Compounding this problem is the slow growth of the labor force, which is only about sixteen percent annually, until the year 2000. This is a much lower growth rate than the annual 26.5 percent during the 1976–1988 period, according to the U.S. Bureau of Labor Statistics.

The primary reason for the slowdown is a decline of births in the early 1970s. The "birth dearth" of that decade, combined with applicant incompetence, yields a shrinking workforce of eighteen-to-twenty-four-year-olds. This shrinkage will persist until nearly the year 2000, bringing about the slowest growth in our labor force since the 1930s, according to the U.S. Labor Department. "This trend is especially troublesome for small businesses that generally hire younger, less-experienced workers," according to a 1991 article in *Nation's Business* magazine.

Indeed, as The American Society for Training and Development declares: "The nation's need for smarter workers is on a collision course with an ill-prepared labor supply. By the year 2000, more than half of America's new jobs will require education beyond high school."

The demands of work and the qualifications for work have changed, and so have the sources of workers. This book identifies new sources for labor, as well as nontraditional, innovative methods of reaching those sources.

Independent businesspeople are being hit from both sides: An increasing demand for labor on one end, and a deficient labor force on the other. One reason for the labor deficiency is that more than forty-three thousand new businesses start up in America each year, the U.S. Labor Department says.

The effect of this situation on American business owners is personal and real. Judy and Alvin Whatley have experienced, firsthand, the negative fallout of the labor crisis. Their company, Interstate Roofing and Sheet Metal, of Coeur d'Alene, Idaho, has suffered a loss of growth potential because of the shortage of qualified workers. New employees tend to dislike the hard work and quit in short order, say the Whatleys.

"We're always startled by the lack of response to our ads for workers, or by the response from people who are woefully under-qualified," confirms Peter F. Burke, vice president of Colahan-Saunders Corporation, a commercial printing firm based in New York, New York.

Compounding the problem is the fact that the independent business owner settles for poorly qualified supervisors, the only kind available from an under-qualified front line. This is aggravated by the fact that jobs have become very specialized.

"Companies want people who are trained on specific computers and word processing packages," says Terry Neese of Neese Personnel Services in Oklahoma City. "The upshot is that qualified people who can fill these requirements are just not there."

Characteristics of low worker competence levels include:

- High absentee rates.
- Rapid job turnover.
- Failure to perform quality work.
- Uncooperative work attitudes.

The Winninger system described in this book shows how to "hire smart" by excluding the unmotivated and the unskilled from the entire process. It will also explain how to bring your employees "up to speed," resulting in significant savings to your business.

I recommend that employers avoid the belief that the problem of finding qualified employees will disappear after the economy becomes healthy.

Kevin R. Hopkins, adjunct senior fellow at the Hudson Institute, made this prediction: "Once we return to a full-strength economy, the worker shortage is going to be just where it was . . . That's not going to change."

Although the ongoing recession and rising unemployment rate may temporarily mask some of the problems associated with these labor difficulties, says Hopkins, "today's economic conditions don't change the basic demographic or skill-level equations . . . ."

The quality level of the people you hire today will determine the future growth of your company.

The state of the nation's economy notwithstanding, innovative and effective hiring techniques will always be a boon to any independent business. Don't write off the possibility that you can find qualified people to work for you and become your future managers. Finding them is *not* impossible. And don't wait until someone quits before you start hiring. Recruitment is a continuous job.

HIRING SMART

Chapter 1

Puzzle Wrapped in a Riddle: How to Find Quality Employees

Running a small or independent business is a tough job. Finding qualified workers is part of that job. Many business owners find themselves stuck in a rut because they seek new employees in the same old places, and often cannot find the time to be creative in recruiting.

Today's labor problem is clearly described by Marilyn Block, executive vice president of The Naisbitt Group, a consulting firm specializing in trend analysis, forecasting and strategic planning. She said: ". . . In the coming decade, as you have more difficulty getting people in at the bottom, you will have a smaller total pool and fewer candidates to move up through the ranks. It's a 'trickle up' theory."

But you can beat the odds. Indeed, there are methods of finding qualified people to fill your positions. Begin with an earnest effort to select qualified people for interviews. You will then be able to hire "the best of the best" because you will have already filtered out the worst. What you must not do is hold a public cattle call. Not only will you waste your time and money, but you will increase the risk of hiring unqualified people.

The trouble with interviewing every applicant is the fact that 70 percent of all hiring decisions involving an interview are based on personal chemistry—instinctive feelings of like or dislike. Few interviewers realize that the very person they dislike may be the best candidate for a given job.

One of the most important techniques in attracting high-quality people to interviews involves approach and timing. Specifically, you must reach prospects who are dissatisfied with their current job and haven't yet begun to seek new employment. If you contact applicants at this stage, you'll have a jump on half the employers in your community.

These are the three stages occupied by all people headed for another job:

1. Dissatisfaction. They know that they are unhappy with their jobs, but their dissatisfaction hasn't progressed to the point where it becomes an ongoing concern.
2. Movement. They begin planning a job search.
3. Active Search. They look for a job.

If you don't prepare by hiring only qualified people at the entry level, you'll end up with unqualified managers later. Here's an example:

A manager gives two weeks notice, so you look among your technicians for the best one to promote to manager. What preparation does that person have for being a manager? None. What training is that person going to receive after he or she becomes a manager? Usually none. Consequently, the new manager spends time doing what he or she is familiar and comfortable with, which is the job he or she was doing before the promotion. That's everything but managing. Further problems will occur because you will now have two people performing the same duties: the new manager and the person who takes over the new manager's former job. Better crank up your recruiting machinery.

Care in recruiting is vital today because each employee in our modern, "lean and mean" companies is more important to the success of the company than they were when staffs were larger. Employees are expected to be more knowledgeable, more productive, and more imaginative than ever before.

They must be creative and motivated to learn. They must be able to offer perceptions about customers, or insights into the production process. These days, an order clerk may be expected to pinch-hit as a salesperson, analyze operations like a consultant, and communicate like a leader.

Brains have replaced brawn as an employee's most valuable asset. By and large, our economy has moved from relying on physical capital (blast furnaces in steel mills, foundries in auto manufacturing companies) to relying on human capital, such as knowledge, experience, talent, and intelligence.

"It's a company's knowledge base—which rests in its employees—that will dictate its success or failure," says Richard Crawford, author of *In the Era of Human Capital*.

Finding qualified people who become loyal to the company, remaining with the firm for decades, may determine success or failure of companies in this knowledge-based economy.

You are what you hire. Your long-term financial success depends upon the quality of your employees. Finding quality employees requires a quality recruiting and hiring process.

Ordinary recruitment methods aren't much more effective than a sandwich board or a town crier standing on a street corner and yelling, "Jobs available! Jobs available!" A "Help Wanted" sign hanging from your plant gate or posted on your front door is likely to attract no more than a bored glance these days, especially if you're offering low-paying jobs with no prestige and little chance for advancement.

If you say that your business can't afford to sustain the disciplined, continuous recruiting process needed to find qualified people, then I say, "You can't afford not to."

Consider the cost of a "mishire": salary, fringe benefits, recruitment and training expenses—all for naught. A salesperson who lasts just six months in an office products dealership costs the company $17,000. This is an estimate based on the calculations of Michael Riordan, president of Riordan and Association, a management consulting firm in Kansas City.

True, that's not a catastrophic number. But your loss is compounded by intangible expenses—time you invested in the employee, lost sales opportunities, and loss of morale on the team. Such intangible costs can amount to seven times your tangible losses. Michael Riordan's calculations have produced this estimate. Tangible and intangible costs of this particular bad hire, he says, amounts to about $136,000. Surprised?

Mike Koether is president of Infincom, a Phoenix, Arizona-based office equipment distributor that maintains five thousand to six thousand customer contacts each month.

For Koether, intangible costs are quite significant: "What looks like a $1,500-a-month hiring mistake becomes a lot more expensive when you multiply that amount times my annual turnover and the number of customers that are let down."

The cruelest cost, however, is the most subtle: The loss of what might have been. That mishired salesperson cost you all the positive things that might have occurred had you hired the perfect candidate: a re-energized sales team, a fresh flow of new product ideas, maybe even your next vice president of operations.

There are hundreds of components in successful hiring. The most important of them—job satisfaction for *present* employees and networking, for example—are described in this book.

To hire well, you must begin with the premise that hiring is an ongoing process, a constant investment of your company's time and energy, whether or not you have a job to fill. The rewards are handsome and, in most cases, far greater than what you expected.

The later you activate the recruiting process, the more rushed the process becomes. This inevitably leads to lower hiring standards, exaggerating a candidate's positive attributes, and overlooking his or her negative ones.

"Recruiting today is not up to snuff," says Joseph Gibbons of Towers Perrin, a New York-based management consulting firm. "Employers must spend more time on the recruiting process so they can be confident of hiring the right individuals."

One advanced recruiting technique for small businesses is "demographic recruiting." Identify population groups in which you are most likely to find recruits and aim your efforts at them. Here's an example:

Conventional wisdom holds that customers for upscale products do not live in my home town of Waterloo, Iowa. But we identified thirty-seven-hundred households—out of a total of thirty thousand—that had net average income of $75,000. This knowledge gave us a big advantage in selling home decorating products.

David Birch, the president of Cognetics, Inc., believes that as the labor market tightens, large corporations become more aggressive about hiring. "We have seen a real slowdown in small business growth related to the shortage of qualified workers," says Birch. ". . . Small firms will slow down relatively more than big firms because they won't be able to compete in the labor market."

As a result, the pool from which small firms can draw workers contracts. A small-business owner, says Birch, is left with three options:

1. Substitute machines for people.
2. Shrink the business.
3. Forget about growing.

We disagree. There is a fourth option:

4. Apply modern, nontraditional methods of finding and hiring qualified people. Then treat them like people so they'll stay.

All of the techniques described in this book I have applied in my businesses. I know that they work.

The future of your company depends not so much upon the quality of the person you can hire as it does upon the quality of the person you interview. That is, attracting highly qualified applicants has a greater influence upon a company's performance than the hiring does. Why? Because the people you hire are more likely to be qualified if the pool of applicants from which they are chosen consists of better-qualified people.

You are what you hire. Your long-term financial success depends upon the quality of your people.

You find quality people with a quality recruiting and hiring process.

Chapter 2

Strategies and Ideas

Ordinary recruitment methods don't work anymore. We don't advocate sky writing or brochures that say "Take this job." We *do* suggest creativity in proactive round-ups of "suspects," converting them into "prospects," and doing it continuously.

Continuous prospecting is a very important recruiting system. Don't wait until your production manager, sales manager, or mail room clerk has jumped to a competitor before you crank up your hiring machinery. Don't wait for an emergency.

"We were reactive," says Jim Fuchs, president of Fuchs Copy Systems, in Milwaukee. "We would suddenly lose an employee, so we'd jump into action and say, 'We've got to hire quickly!' Six candidates would come in and we'd hire one. Chances are, the person wouldn't be a good fit, because we hired the best of the worst. We hired out of desperation."

Targeted Recruiting Plan

Focus upon people who fit a Central Demographic Model (CDM) for the position to be filled. The CDM describes the demographic group in which you expect the most qualified prospects to be found.

Let's say that you want to hire a sales representative for an interior decorating and design company. Write a CDM that consists of attributes such as these:

Sample Demographic Model (CDM)

A-B-C Decorating Company
Central Demographic Model
Sales Representative

Age:	Thirty-five to forty-five.
	Interior design is a second career.
	Children.
Home value:	More than $100,000.
	Well-networked in the community.
	Compensation from job would not be primary family income.

To contact people with these characteristics, buy a mailing list of owners of homes valued at more than $100,000, or a list of people in your community who subscribe to *Vogue* or *Lear's* magazines (read largely by women interested in fashion, design, and the arts). Many of the people who buy these magazines probably match your CDM.

Let's say that you lure a number of potential job applicants who match your CDM. Before you invite them in for a test and an interview, create a "rating schedule." This schedule should consist of all major personal characteristics, with a range of points assigned to each characteristic. It's a rating schedule for *your* job, not for similar jobs in other same-sized companies.

To equip yourself to write a rating schedule, do a job analysis such as this:

SAMPLE JOB ANALYSIS

Telemarketing Inc.
Job Analysis
Crew Leader

Ability to analyze results	1 2 3 4 5
Ability to delegate responsibility	1 2 3 4 5
Communication skills	1 2 3 4 5
Leadership abilities	1 2 3 4 5
Professionalism	1 2 3 4 5
Telephone etiquette	1 2 3 4 5
Training: knowledge, capability	1 2 3 4 5
Willingness to learn	1 2 3 4 5

"Break the job down into its important components — specific desired behavior and skills," advises Therese Hoff

Macan, an assistant professor of psychology at the University of Missouri, St. Louis, who specializes in employment interview research.

Follow the rating schedule as you interview. Write down a point value beside each item in the schedule. For a junior-level administrative assistant's job, for instance, you might create a rating schedule that includes telephone research ability, written communication skills, and experience in your industry.

If your Targeted Recruiting Plan is well executed, you will reach a demographic group made up of people qualified for *your* jobs. The next step is finding people within the demographic group who actually meet your hiring criteria. You must hand-pick individuals to become your "prospects," those who have advanced from the "suspect" stage. When the only people you ever interview are hand-picked suspects, then you will be in a position to skim the whipped cream off the dessert instead of settling for the crumbs that fall from the table.

If you succeed in the "finding" process, you would be hard-pressed to hire the wrong person. With ten high-quality suspects who want to work for you, you could be the world's worst interviewer and still succeed in hiring a qualified employee.

Here are a few unconventional ideas for finding applicants:

Idea One Offer job search assistance and free career counseling through Welcome Wagon and other newcomers groups. New residents may appreciate your offer more than the usual "dollars off" coupons and free advertising gimmicks. You might also contact the corporate relocation departments of the local offices of national real estate brokers. More and more realtors provide career assistance for spouses when only husband or wife has a job in a new community. Propose that they retain you to do the work for them.

Idea Two   Dickie Dees is the Canadian version of the US Good Humor man. Both are bicycle or small-truck vendors of ice cream novelty items during the summer. Both face an annual challenge, attracting boys thirteen to eighteen years of age to fill all of the summer delivery positions.

The Canadian company, Dickie Dees, has no trouble filling the positions, now that they invite all boys of the required age to a free concert just before the ice cream selling season begins. The company gets backstage passes from radio stations and donates them to the boys.

Boys who are hired are told that they can earn bonuses, including low-priced record album covers, and name-brand tape and compact disc players.

Idea Three   Print a "Wanted" poster—a flyer asking people to apply for the position. Devise imaginative ways to distribute the posters. You might print it on milk cartons, or offer supermarkets a penny per flyer that their baggers stuff into shoppers' grocery bags. How about hiring high school kids to hand out the posters to motorists at stop lights during rush hour, or employing an independent delivery service to hang them on doorknobs? The trick is to be unconventional. What are *your* ideas?

Slutzky's method for weeding out applicants for telephone work is to run a small ad in which he invites people to call a phone number. When people call the number, they hear a long message describing the job and the suggestion that they call back to record a pitch for themselves. This method eliminates those who don't call back, either because they don't like the job or they feel unqualified for it. The messages that *are* left allow Slutzky to evaluate a caller's suitability for telephone work.

While applicants are asked to leave the names of three people who would nominate them for the position, Slutzky advises against asking them to detail their years of schooling, their last six jobs, and what they do in their free time. Even application forms and resumes are discouraged. The reason for doing so is probably unreliability. Slutsky apparently feels that today's applicant is expert at giving disinformation and concealing derogatory details.

Lynn Taylor, vice president of Robert Half International, a Menlo Park, California, recruiting firm, exposes tricks of the resume-preparation trade: "The candidate who says she 'supervised a department' is likely to be talking about a very small department. If it was a full-time staff of eighty-five, she'd be more likely to spell that out.

"Be wary of lengthy descriptions of education and puffed-up personal sections. (How can someone with that many hobbies have time or real enthusiasm for work?) Too many phrases like 'had exposure to,' 'assisted with,' or 'have a knowledge of,' signal that the applicant lacks the hands-on experience you're looking for."

I've learned that for every ten people interviewed, three real prospects emerge; and with those three applicants, one is likely to become a genuine prospect. I've also learned that after identifying a prospect, I need about three interview sessions. Occasionally things don't work out and I must begin again.

Devote Time to Hiring

Let's say that you have ten positions to fill in your front line. Be prepared to talk with no fewer than one hundred applicants. At forty-five minutes per interview, you will invest a hundred hours in a hundred people. Most owners and managers spend about sixty to seventy hours a week at work (about 250 hours per month). So, during a month when you're recruiting, you can spend 40 percent of your time conducting interviews.

By now you may be reaching for the aspirin bottle and trying to devise ways to add days to the calendar. You must, however, face the fact that recruiting requires commitment, much time, and a lot of effort. Look at it this way: If one hundred hours of effective recruiting leads to an increase of 12 to 18 percent in profit margin because you hire a star, wouldn't you be happy to invest that time?

Finding highly qualified people to help you in your business can increase profit even more than that.

Thomas H. Melohn, president, CEO and part owner of North American Tool & Die Company in San Leandro, California, says: "With our strong belief in the importance of our employees, it's axiomatic that we hire only the best. We hire a certain kind of person—a decent person who cares about himself, his family, and his company. The person must be honest, willing to speak up, and curious—be it as a sweeper, machine operator, plant foreman, or office manager.

"That's why I interview each prospective employee myself," says Melohn. "My purpose is to determine if the candidate will fit into the (company) family. Perhaps that concept seems old-fashioned, but to us it's critically important. Evaluation and interviewing is a lot of work, but the results are well worth it."

One important feature of the recruiting system proposed in this book is continuous prospecting.

ഗ്ര

Don't wait for emergencies before beginning the recruiting process.

ഗ്ര

When the only people you ever interview are hand-picked "suspects," then you will be in a position to skim the whipped cream off the dessert instead of settling for the crumbs that fall from the table.

ഗ്ര

Three of every ten people, or one of three people interviewed, become applicants in most situations.

Chapter 3

Secret Hiring Bait of Small Businesses: Job Satisfaction

Your organization probably has a reputation among residents of your community. People rate your company as either "a good place to work" or "a bad place to work." Members of today's labor force will call it a *good* place to work if your employees:

- Have a chance to use valued skills.
- Are allowed to solve problems through their own efforts.
- Receive recognition when they perform well.
- Control their own work strategies.
- Are given a chance to offer input to discussions that affect them and their work.

- Receive tasks that require a great deal of effort to complete.
- Work with others on the job.

In other words, people tend to enjoy opportunities to influence situations, to feel important, to use valued skills and abilities, and to be recognized or rewarded for contributions.

Most of these job features are seen more often in small organizations than in large corporations. (That should be encouraging.)

Don't surrender to big company hiring power. You, too, have certain advantages. If you pay employees a fair wage and they feel like members of a team, then the most important remaining features of a job are the chance to learn, the opportunity to apply valued skills, and the right to make decisions about how work gets done.

Make this message part of your recruiting story: "A smaller company can provide greater job satisfaction than most large companies." You'll find that to be a powerful hiring pitch.

I've had people come to me and say, "Look, Tom, I don't care what you pay me. I just want to be able to take my daughter to school at nine o'clock in the morning and pick her up at three o'clock in the afternoon. I'll be glad to come in at seven a.m. and work until six p.m. if I can just have a little time off to take her to school and to pick her up."

Make sure that you ask applicants what they expect from a job. If you don't satisfy an applicant's expectations, you won't solve your staffing problem for long. It's that simple.

Your competition for qualified employees isn't always the business down the street. It's the prospect's expectations.

The chance to satisfy personal needs and to balance work and leisure pursuits is important to many people. Here are some significant personal needs that your prospect may have:

- A feeling of growth in the job.
- A sense of career potential.
- A feeling of individual responsibility.
- Good relationships with customers.

Good relationships with employers are important, too. The era of "boss-as-dictator" is gone. These days, an employer should also be a coach, mentor, advisor, listener, designer, and facilitator to his or her employee.

Another change in the working world today is the increased appreciation of creativity. The responsibility of management is seen as hiring the best employees and creating an environment that will allow them to do their best work. Much more of the job than before is left to workers as individuals and in groups.

The most popular management styles today discard strict hierarchy, encourage individual creativity, and foster trust. Creativity and initiative are recognized and encouraged.

One of the best-known applications of this style, a model of humanistic management, is active at Saturn Corporation in Spring Hill, Tennessee. The company developed a work ethic that promotes personal job satisfaction.

The new ethic sentences sharp status distinctions and adversarial relationships between bosses and employees to the same chapter in the history of business that deals with feudalism and serfs.

The focus of the Saturn culture is job design that yields job satisfaction. There are no time clocks at Saturn Corporation plants. All employees are organized into teams of twelve to fifteen. Supervisors are advisors. Employees are empowered to contribute to the entire process of achieving a work team's goals. Every employee is on salary, like managers.

Fear still is used widely by American business managers to induce conformity. But, fortunately the fear style of management has acquired a bad reputation. Creativity is less often squelched by an atmosphere of fear—fear of a dictatorial boss's whims, fear of doing anything except that which one has been *told* to do, or fear of doing anything enterprising because of repercussions that would occur in the event of failure.

Business owners and managers intent upon building their companies' reputations as a good place to work should know what people are afraid of. Primarily, they are afraid of having their images tarnished—of "looking bad." That's the well-informed opinion of Larry Wilson, management training guru and founder of Pecos River Learning Center in Santa Fe, New Mexico.

In his colorful way, Wilson elaborates: "People are not as afraid of dying as they are of looking bad *while* dying."

People shouldn't work in fear and under stress. Work should be fun. When it *is* fun and gratifying, people willingly work hard and well.

FLATTER ORGANIZATIONS

Wilson says: "All of us grew up with sort of a have-to, fear-based motivational system, going all the way back to Caesar. That system gave rise to a pyramid-type hierarchy in which the person at the top gave the orders, the many workers at the bottom were expected to do as they were told, and the managers in between were to make sure they did it."

That system assumes that one person at the top has all the answers. In today's complicated, fast-paced world, that's just not possible.

That's why we need flatter, less pyramid-like, organizations with employees who are encouraged to think and to come up with their own ideas.

"Managing" is thus shifted from the executive suite to the operational level where everyone is now a manager of his own situation. When problems arise, each employee has authority to determine appropriate action and to see to it that the action is carried out by himself/herself or with the help of others.

"We're going to be so short of workers by the end of the decade, particularly information service workers, that companies that try to manage in the old top-down, hierarchical, drill-sergeant way are just doomed," says James Autry of Meredith Corporation.

Eliminating fear among employees helps to develop a good company reputation for your prospective employees.

A mechanism as complex as a human mind cannot function effectively under a cloud of constant supervision and predetermined action that constitutes the traditional, now waning, American management system. Such a cloud is noticed by the community from which you draw your employees and by the people who fit your CDM.

Make the opportunity for personal satisfaction and fulfillment at work one of your primary messages to potential employees and you'll go a long way toward solving your recruitment problem.

Many employees still are badgered by fear, though business consultants counsel against fear, following the lead of W. Edwards Deming's ideas. Deming, who died in 1994, promulgated fourteen points for achieving quality and lowering costs. He used them to teach the Japanese to dominate one industry after another in the global marketplace before his ideas were accepted in the United States.

Deming's eighth principle was that of eliminating fear. He maintained that driving fear out of an organization is the indispensable prelude to successful application of any of his other thirteen modern management imperatives.

For all the crustiness that was a prominent part of his reputation, Deming alone correctly identified fear as the basis of all barriers to improving a company. He knew that, good intentions aside, people who work for a living will bow to the system that employs them, and he thought that was a crime.

The *significance* of a low-fear workplace in which employees are respected and their ideas sought and valued is its *value in recruitment*. A company's reputation as "a good place to work" skyrockets when it becomes well-known for encouraging people to *be* who they *are*. This environment becomes a strong attraction to potential employees—an advantage over competitors in the job market.

Additional characteristics of the fearless workplace that attract job applicants are: nurture, support, collaboration, cooperation, facilitation of personal growth and development, trust, and open and honest communication.

An excessively heavy "cloud of supervision" is noticed by the community from which you draw future employees and by the people who fit your Central Demographic Model. Opportunity for personal job satisfaction should be one of your primary messages to potential employees. Do this and you'll make great strides toward solving your recruitment problem.

The consequences of management by fear provide ample justification for reducing it. Consider elimination of even some of the consequences to be a bonus added to your enhanced attractiveness to job hunters.

Here is a synopsis of consequences listed by several famed consultants, including Wilson and Deming, who say that employees driven by fear:

- Hang on to what they already know, and resist new information and change.
- Do just enough to get by.
- Are cautious.
- Value comfort and learn apathy.
- Hide mistakes.
- Repeat old patterns, even though they were ineffective.
- Conduct turf wars.
- Buy into the win–lose orientation.

Tom Monaghan, who founded and built the Domino's Pizza empire and became a billionaire, said in 1992 that he would sell his empire to devote more time to his family and to his personal relationships and satisfaction.

It seems as though he had become haunted by a bible verse he was taught as a youngster: "A camel can pass through the eye of a needle easier than a rich man can get into heaven."

In his younger days, Monaghan spent his money freely. He was an avid fan of the Detroit Tigers baseball team, and bought them. He paid $25 million for a wooded retreat. He purchased sports cars, artwork, gems, and houses. He said that he bought things to impress others. But, none of those things made *him* happy.

Abraham Maslow, the father of humanistic psychology, postulated a hierarchy of human needs. Most basic (the lowest-level needs), he said, are physiological needs. These are followed by the need for security, social needs, esteem needs and, finally, the highest need, a need for "self-actualization."

Self-actualization incorporates David McClelland's theory of achievement but is defined in broader terms. Maslow's theory of the hierarchy of needs postulates that a higher need will become active only if the lower needs are sufficiently satisfied. Our actions are basically rational activities by which we expect to fulfill successive levels of needs.

Maslow defined self-actualization as everything that one is capable of becoming. Business' role should be to help employees be everything they are capable of becoming. This is the way to boost productivity and product quality. *Self-actualization* refers to the whole person, not just to the part of a person that earns a living.

People enabled and inspired by humane, ethical management (and rewarding jobs) work harder and better. They express a greater proportion of their personal potential in terms of quality, creativity, and productivity.

As we climb Maslow's hierarchy of needs beyond survival and a sense of belonging, we come to the status-ego needs and finally to self-actualization. *Most of us spend only a small part of our lives in the self-actualizing phase.*

Psychologist Frederick Herzberg, a professor at Case Western University, has developed a two factor theory of motivation. It distinguishes between hygienic factors (largely corresponding to Maslow's lower needs—physiological, security, social) and motivators (Maslow's higher needs—esteem and self-actualization). Hygienic factors have only the potential to motivate negatively—*to demotivate*. Only the motivators have the potential to motivate positively.

Victor Vroom, well-known management scholar, has formalized the role of "expectancy" in motivation. He sees people as being *pulled* by the expectancy of a result from their actions, most often consciously. He opposes "drive" theories, which (in accordance with Sigmund Freud's theories) view people as being *pushed* by inside forces—often unconscious ones.

Geert Hofstede is a management consultant who heads international research and program development at Management Decisions, Inc., in Darien, Connecticut. He believes that Maslow's hierarchy puts self-actualization (achievement) *plus* esteem above social needs, which are, in turn, above security needs. "This, however, is not the description of a universal human motivation process," he writes. "It is the description of a *value system*, the value system of the U.S. middle class to which the author belonged."

The "humanization" concept, including satisfaction in work and enthusiasm for work, may have received a boost from the call by President Bush for a "kinder, gentler nation." But still, many Americans identify with the "me" mentality. Individualism is still a very strong feature of the American personality.

Nevertheless, "The Great American TV Poll," conducted by the *Lifetime* television show in 1991, found that goals represented by the "me" mentality, such as personal ambition, now rank at the bottom of a list of values most important to a survey group. At the top are "we" values such as a happy marriage, friendships, religion, and good health.

Life often becomes happier when we abandon headlong, self-centered pursuits of power and wealth and focus upon self-fulfillment on the job, with family, and through participation in social and leisure activities that satisfy us.

When people use their personal lives to rejuvenate themselves for work, not only does life become happier, but work becomes more productive.

We've tried to achieve quality without humanizing of work.

We've tried to boost productivity without first humanizing work.

We've tried technology and financial manipulation and research and control management techniques such as Management by Objection (MBO)—and MBAs from Ivy League schools without first trying humanization.

Now it's time to try *humanization*.

We've never really tried to influence people to *want to* do their best work *willingly*.

People enjoy opportunities to influence situations, to feel important, to use skills and abilities, and to be recognized or rewarded for contributions.

If you pay employees a fair wage and they feel like a member of the team, then the most important features of a job for them are a chance to learn, an opportunity to apply valued skills, and the right to make decisions about how they do their work.

Your organization is a good place to work if your employees are allowed to solve problems by themselves.

Chapter 4

Recruiting: A Job for You

The job of recruitment is so important that the top person in any organization should allot a large chunk of time to it every day. Recruiting work should be done as naturally and frequently as taking the morning tour around the plant or the store.

"Center of Influence" is the name of the recruiting routine used by Tom Garrison and his retail managers. Garrison is president of Brown, Moore and Flint, a Dallas-based food broker. When Garrison meets someone whom he thinks would make a good employee, he engages that person in conversation about his food brokerage business. "If the person is enthusiastic," says Garrison, "and I see that he or she understands what I'm saying, then I explain why Brown, Moore and Flint is a good place to work."

Garrison describes the qualities he looks for in a job candidate and asks his newly anointed "center of influence" to watch for people who fit that description. Garrison's managers have been "seeding" the area with centers of influence for seven years. The result is four or five calls a week regarding potential candidates.

Good centers of influence may come from anywhere. Garrison's own clients are some of his best recruiters. Sometimes these "recruiters" are so taken with the company that they apply for jobs themselves. (A similar technique—Talent Scout Cards—is discussed in the next chapter, "Employees As Recruiters.") The leader of the company should be the leader of the recruiting process. He or she should assume responsibility for continuous recruiting and should freshen the plan with new ideas. Public appearances are one way for the leader to develop and maintain a high profile and positive reputation in his or her community. He or she should write and rehearse a talk about their type of business, then offer the speech to service, professional, and social groups.

Jim Lind, proprietor of Jim Lind Amoco, a large Waterloo, Iowa, service station, is a master of continuous high-profile recruiting. "Among my sixty part-time people, I have a 30 percent annual turnover due to employee graduation from high school," says Lind. "So I keep working at recruitment. I want the best kids working for me. I reach out. I sponsor high-profile school athletic events, and I recruit high school students through my own seminars on business concepts. This also promotes word of mouth about my company."

As a result of this kind of proactive recruiting, most of Lind's employees are "networked" to him. He does no employment advertising. And recruitment doesn't stop once a person is hired. On the contrary, the strategy builds. Through on-the-job training, reasonable wages, college assistance, and subsequent job recommendations, Lind demonstrates to the entire community that his firm is a great place to work.

The Lind and Garrison recruiting techniques work for them. The strategies reflect their company's needs. They take advantage of opportunities that exist in their communities.

Recruiting is so important that the top person in any organization should spend a significant amount of time with it everyday. Recruiting should be part of business culture, something done as naturally and frequently as taking the morning tour around the plant or the store.

If you compete for workers with only the offer of a salary and benefits, cost of labor may outstrip company profit.

You are less likely to find qualified applicants during a staffing panic. Your best prospects will be found when your company is fully staffed, when you have time for effective search and evaluation.

Don't depend entirely upon "Help Wanted" advertising. About 83 percent of the workforce *cannot* be reached by that means.

Don't entice job applicants with unrealistic promises of success and affluence.

Chapter 5

Employees As Recruiters

The director of human resources at Quaker Fabric Corporation, of Fall River, Massachusetts, was brainstorming methods to motivate his employees to refer qualified prospects. Suddenly it hit him. Half of Quaker's employees speak only Portuguese and pine for a return to Portugal. Why not offer them a trip back home as grand prize in a drawing? Their eligibility begins when they recommend prospects. An added incentive would be to pay $100 per referral.

Employee referral programs are among the most successful means of finding loyal, productive employees, especially when the goal is to reproduce the makeup of a current workforce.

There are two key ways to increase participation: (1) Offer incentives that vary with the level of the position to be filled, and the difficulty of filling that position. (2) Promote the incentive program with both current and new employees during orientation.

Who knows your needs better than your own people? Your current employees are familiar with the workplace and are well-qualified to screen candidates for personal characteristics that meld into the job environment. Furthermore, your employees have a stake in the candidates they refer: to some extent, their own standing in the firm is on the line. They won't risk it by pushing dubious choices, even for cash incentives.

Pay your employees enough to motivate them to actively look for prospects. Here's a suggested payment schedule for nominations of frontline employees:

Level 1: $25 for an applicant that earns a third interview.

Level 2: Additional $50 for a hire.

Level 3: Final $75 bonus if new employee stays at least twelve months.

Paying employees $150 for one new employee that stays for a year may seem like a lot of money, but it's no more than a "tip" compared with fees charged by employment agencies and head hunters, who charge 30 percent of annual salary, and sometimes more. (A system of partial payments in stages tends to discourage blatant gold-digging.)

A well-known theme park in New Jersey pays $50 to the referring employee and $50 to the new hire. The University National Bank and Trust Company, located in

Palo Alto, California, pays its current employees a "referral fee" for referring outstanding former co-workers from previous jobs. "Our goal," says vice president Ann Sonnenberg, "is to hire genuinely nice people who are very capable and who enjoy helping others."

Businesses that rely upon third-party recruiters and recruitment agencies discover that, when they remove the middlemen, recruitment expenses drop dramatically *without* reducing the quality of the applicants.

A staff recruiting program is a reliable source of new employees. Your staff is aware that you are trusting them to help you recruit, and they know that you are investing cold cash. According to one theory, a sense of fairness usually prevents them from sending you anyone poorly qualified. Some organizations use hiring committees made up of both executives and employees, each of whom serves for six months. Committee members are constantly on the alert for prospects—anyone who impresses them. Members obtain the person's name and phone number. They list only prospects that they have seen in action.

Another way to involve employees in the recruitment process is to have them distribute Talent Scout Cards to people who perform at a high level of quality. Talent Scout Cards are a little larger than business cards. Your company name, a twenty-four-hour toll-free phone number, and a sell line appear on the front of the cards; a concise summary of jobs appears on the back. Another recruitment method is to enlist the aid of former employees—retirees included—who left the organization on good terms.

About 80 percent of all service workers are recruited through job networks made up of current, satisfied employees, according to Lee Bowes in her book *No One Need Apply* (Boston, Massachusetts: Harvard Business School Press, 1987). That makes an employee referral and reward system worth a try.

Employee referral programs are among the most successful means of finding loyal, productive employees, especially when the goal is to reproduce the makeup of a current workforce.

A staff recruiting program is a reliable source of new employees because employees are aware that you are trusting them to help you recruit. A sense of fairness prevents them from sending you anyone who is poorly qualified.

Ask employees to distribute Talent Scout Cards to people they observe performing at a high level of quality.

Chapter 6

Hire Your Own Employees Before Someone Else Does

"My name is Pete. I work at a little electronics plant on the edge of town. I've been there for three years now, doing about the same thing I did the week I started.

"It just occurred to me that I never heard my supervisor or anybody else talk about opportunities for promotion. I like the work and the people here, but maybe the only way to get ahead in life is to get a better job with another company."

This twenty-eight-year-old graduate of a good trade school has the qualities that employers seek. He's hardworking, eager to learn, smart, and creative. But he wants the opportunity to learn, to be creative, and to advance.

This situation is the same for millions of other people employed in thousands of small- and medium-sized manufacturing and service companies. The employees eventually leave for greener pastures, even though they like their job and their co-workers.

"Surveys reveal that the number one complaint of employees is that they never know when there are promotion opportunities within the company; there's no succession or career planning," says Barbara Sanfilippo, consultant for the Oakland, California firm Romano and Sanfilippo, a specialist in quality service and sales culture development.

It is very possible that the employee you need to fill that vacant position may already be on your payroll. Cataloging and developing the knowledge and skills of your employees today will very likely pay off in the future. Here is some action that can be taken:

- Hold coaching sessions to determine which employees really want more responsibility and money.
- Post jobs notices internally before seeking applicants outside the company. Promote from within whenever possible.
- Keep your staff informed of opportunities for advancement with a frequently updated "Future Needs Function Chart" that emphasizes steps toward promotion. Distribute a "Learning Opportunity List" to your employees (see below).

Staff Development

The process of internal promotion as a means of solving staffing problems begins with a staff development program designed to train employees for advancement. As part of that program, publish an annual Learning Opportunity List. It should include:

- Skill-building seminars or classes—make it company policy to invest in the staging of employee learning opportunities.
- Schedule of events, activities, seminars and classes available in the community—obtain information from the Chamber of Commerce, community and technical colleges, and other organizations.

Your company will benefit when you provide your staff with such opportunities to develop social and personal skills. When employees apply these skills on the job, they enhance the value of the services or product. They also win customer goodwill, which brings with it greater customer loyalty, more frequent purchases, and a higher purchase amount per visit. Not only does the company come out ahead, but the individual employee benefits, too; their new skills cause them to become more successful, more satisfied, and less likely to leave.

Original Research Corporation (ORC) in Chicago conducts the ORC II Merit University. The company, which employs three hundred fifty people, contacts the purchasers of new and used motor vehicles and asks them to evaluate the service they received from the sellers. ORC provides the survey results to their clients, most of whom are auto dealers.

The ORC University offers more than two hundred courses. Subjects covered: using a calculator; company history; purpose of work; balancing a checkbook and memo-writing and interviewing for jobs. The curriculum also includes training in business skills, such as dressing for success; imparting ideas to management; ways to propose change; and tips on writing a thank you note, running a copy machine, and taking a phone message.

The university also trains employees in life skills, such as preparing a family budget, and choosing between fixed-rate financing and revolving credit.

The ORC employees, most of them college students who work part-time, are trained for success on company time. This training develops loyalty in students who are preparing for jobs in a tight labor market. Some of them apply for permanent jobs with ORC.

Another example of ongoing staff development is a program at a major theme park. The park organization makes it crystal clear to new employees that one must start at the bottom to reach the top.

They're told that pushing brooms, taking tickets, or giving directions to rest rooms are duties that lead to positions as staff supervisors or managers. When a person is hired for frontline employment at this prestigious park, almost two days are devoted to teaching its traditions, goals, values, and philosophies. It is here that fledglings learn to soar. They become aware that life at *this place* can be more than a job. It can be a career.

The Company builds a strong sense of culture in its employees—a sense of values and standards that leads to loyalty and pride. There's a lesson here for *any* business of *any* size. This company has earned the right to boast because of its extremely low employee turnover rate— only 22 percent. Turnover at most theme parks is about one-hundred percent. Management turnover here is even less—about 6 percent.

Coaching

The transitional phase between training and promotion is coaching. In coaching sessions you learn who has potential and who wants to be upwardly mobile.

I try to spend at least a half hour in a coaching session with each member of my staff, weekly. In these sessions I screen their work and point out problems. We also talk about projects and challenges. And we brainstorm, looking for learning opportunities.

As the editors of *Business Week* magazine wrote in a special section on employing the disabled (October 28, 1991 issue), "The evidence is overwhelming that people, not machines, are the driving force behind economic growth today." By spending time on hiring the best possible employees, you are harnessing the driving forces behind the growth of your business—the knowledge, abilities, and enthusiasm of people.

Future Needs Chart

Post your Future Needs/Function Chart with its list of job openings in the staff lounge or meeting room. The chart should show steps required for promotion in terms of knowledge, skill and experience. It *does* motivate employees to work harder and better by giving them direction and offering them a reward.

Every business, regardless of size, should implement a type of futures charting. A Future Needs/Function Chart motivates people to work harder and better by giving them direction and offering a reward for their efforts.

Here is an example of a Future Needs/Function Chart for a small- to medium-size insurance office:

ABC INSURANCE COMPANY
FUTURE NEEDS/FUNCTION CHART

Position	Future Need Opportunitiy	Functions	Requirements
Receptionist	office director	scheduling appointments and meetings	typing: sixty wpm
			dictation
		typing, dictation, reports, claims	friendly, professional telephone skills
		answer telephone	attention to detail, figures
		process mail	
		message distribution	proven ability to work under pressure in busy office

JOB DESCRIPTION

Job descriptions are the foundation for your company's internal staff development and promotion activities.

Writing a job description may seem like a bureaucratic nuisance—one that might be categorized with parking tickets and tax returns. However, we're not referring to the standard, nebulous, all-purpose "duties list," but rather something that includes purpose, objectives, standards, and job philosophy. Preparing this kind of a job description gives you, the employer, an intimate feeling for the requirements of a job. When you meet the person who's qualified for a particular position, you recognize her or him immediately.

Without such a "blueprint," managers often end up hiring a candidate only because they like the person, because the individual had a firm handshake, or on the basis of previous job experience. Screening must be much more thorough than that.

"Most often we make the mistake of hiring in our own image," says TravCorps' Bruce Male.

Before Male began considering applicants for one key position, he created a job description that dramatically altered the kind of person he would hire to be the manager of TravCorps' growing information systems department.

"Initially, I thought that I needed someone with the technical mastery that *I* value," recalls Male.

But in writing the job description and defining the position's purpose and objectives, Male concluded that he needed someone who could develop a department. Technical skill was necessary; but, to successfully develop the growing department, the new manager also would need the "soft" skills of a nurturer and a communicator.

A clear, succinct job description clarifies job objectives and helps lead you to the right candidate.

One challenge you face with a "promotion from within" policy is to live up to your promises. If you say that you plan to advance employees from frontline to supervisory or mid-management positions, then do so. Before you place one more classified ad, see if there's a qualified employee waiting patiently for promotion right there in your company.

A business owner or manager who follows these suggestions can fill at least 10 to 20 percent of open positions by recruiting from within. That's a good start to solving your staffing problems.

The employee you need to fill a vacant position may already be on your payroll.

By spending time on hiring the best possible employees, you harness the driving force behind the growth of your business—the knowledge, abilities, and enthusiasm of people.

A business owner or manager who does the things suggested in this chapter can fill at least 10 to 20 percent of open positions by recruiting from within.

Chapter 7

New Ways to Use Employment Agencies

"**I** got it."

    As far as Ned's wife was concerned, those words were not spoken; they were *sung*.

At breakfast that morning, Ned had been staring at his plate, hardly eating. A quick "Good morning" was all he'd said to ten-year-old Sean, as the boy pulled his chair up to the table. Ned's wife had realized that he was tense, worried, and thoughtful. His job interview had been scheduled for ten a.m. Now, here he was on the phone, calling just after the final interview with the best news possible: "I got it."

Ned deserved a lot of credit for having gotten the job. He'd shown enough savvy about job hunting to ask every personnel and human resources person, every owner and general manager he'd seen, to suggest companies that might be hiring. One of those references finally paid off.

That kind of networking is usually the fastest way to find a job. Employers, too, benefit from tapping into networks (see Chapter 13) when they search for employees. One good strategy is to give vendor reps your business card with a message penned on the back: "Looking for (specify type of employee)." Use vendor representatives as missionaries to the job market. They will spread the word among their clients that you are looking for a production manager, a mail room supervisor, or a receptionist who's knowledgeable about software.

During his job hunt, Ned learned that the personnel agency business has changed. Chief among the changes is a reduction in agency fees—about 20 percent (down from 30 percent) of a new employee's starting annual salary is the cost of an agency's services in finding a new employee. Some agencies now charge by the hour, resulting in a total cost that's less than the twenty-percent fee. Other agencies offer "contingency recruiting," which means you're not charged anything if they don't find you an employee that you're satisfied with. Then there are agencies that restrict their work to research. They send you the candidate names and qualifications; you take it from there. These agencies will also videotape candidates in distant locations, if you request it.

Check with agencies in your local area to determine which services they provide. You may even learn about other new, inexpensive services. Be sure to ask for, and to check, references before using any *new* agency.

Electronic network recruitment is a new service available to employers in search of employees. This enables you to use your own computer to consult a data bank of job candidates' resumes. One of these electronic data base services is Connexion (800-338-3282).

"Companies are inundated with resumes," says Barbara L. Thomas, president of Peterson's Connexion Services in Princeton, New Jersey. "In many cases, they are saying that it is too difficult to deal with. That can make a service like Connexion very attractive.

"Filling positions is going to become a much more creative activity," she explains. "Companies are going to want individuals who have a broader range of experience, who can function with a smaller and more agile staff. We provide such people."

You can reach Connexion on the Internet at **petersons.com.**

Use vendor representatives as missionaries to the job market. Give vendor reps your card with your labor needs written on the back.

Some agencies charge by the hour for their services. Others charge nothing if they don't find an employee that you're satisfied with. This procedure is called "contingency recruiting."

Research agencies will provide you with job candidate names and qualifications, as well as a videotape of candidates in distant locations.

CHAPTER 8

HOW TO HIRE WOMEN: REDUCE STRESS IN THEIR LIVES

It's eight o'clock and the sounds of coughing, shuffling feet, moving chairs, and the typical conversational buzz have subsided. The Orion meeting room of the Civic Center is now quiet.

In a moment, a program developed by the Business Roundtable will begin. The Roundtable is an organization of business entrepreneurs in the Minneapolis–St. Paul area. Its primary purpose is to help individual members meet challenges by pooling their expertise and focusing it upon a specific problem. The Roundtable sometimes assembles authorities to present programs on a particular topic, as it has done tonight.

Six participants in the program are sitting at a long table on the stage, under bright klieg lights, facing the audience. Roger Phillips, this year's Roundtable chairman, walks onto the stage and greets his audience from the podium. "Our subject tonight, as you know, is 'How to Make It Easy for Mothers to Return to Work.' We're honored to have with us several very knowledgeable people. Let me introduce them to you." Phillips introduces his six participants:

- Sophie Dermatis, a working mother and counselor for the Massachusetts Office for Children.
- Barney Olmstead, co-director of New Ways to Work, a San Francisco non-profit group that helps people create flexible employment situations.
- Felice Schwartz, president of Catalyst, a New York non-profit organization that she founded thirty years ago to help secure part-time jobs for the housebound women of her "Feminine Mystique" generation (a term coined by feminist Betty Friedan in her celebrated book *Feminine Mystique*). Schwartz is the author of *Breaking with Tradition* (Warner Books, 1992).
- Kevin Hopkins of The Hudson Institute, a public policy research center located in Indianapolis, Indiana.
- Herta Loeser, co-director of Career Advisory Services of Cambridge, Massachusetts.
- Barbara Sanfilippo, consultant, Romano & Sanfilippo, Oakland, California.

"We believe that many mothers in this community would work if we would make it possible for them to do so," says Phillips. "You could say that this community's mothers have it within their power to solve the staffing problems of our members—and also to fill other jobs in this community. Let's start by discussing what our panel participants can do to make it easier for mothers to gain employment. Mr. Hopkins, will you begin?"

Hopkins turns to address the audience. "Many women have temporarily dropped out of the workforce to raise children, or to accommodate a husband's career. Employers know they're out there, but they don't know how to hire them. The thing to do is facilitate their transition back to part-time or full-time employment.

"We know that the reason many women don't return to work is the high cost of child care. There's not much sense in working if you pay four-fifths of your income to child-care fees. So here's an opportunity. Provide day-care facilities at your business location or off-site, or give employees child-care allowances. If you do this, an army of applicants is likely to descend upon you."

The Polaroid Corporation in Cambridge, Massachusetts, uses a voucher system to subsidize up to 70 percent of each employee's day-care costs. The exact amount depends upon need and income. Parents make their own day-care arrangements.

"You can also offer a child-care benefits package," suggests Hopkins. "Packages provided by most companies provide between $1.50 and $3 per hour to workers who enroll their children in certified day-care facilities. Anything that you can do to help a mother care for and nurture her children will help you in the job market.

"ABT Associates, a social research and consulting firm based in Cambridge, Massachusetts, rents space on its premises to an independent day-care center called Children's Village," notes Hopkins. "It gives ABT families priority on its waiting list, but it also serves other families. I'm suggesting that you start a day-care operation and accept *anyone's* children, thereby making the operation self-sufficient or even profitable.

"Just being considerate of mothers' needs, even if you don't assist with day care, can help attract or keep a worker. Recognize, for instance, that it's just as important for a mother to stay home because her child is ill as it is to stay home because she's sick herself."

Barbara Sanfilippo nods in agreement with Hopkins. "Many of these women want to go back to work, and many who are now working don't want to quit. The problem is that they have children. More women are taking on jobs and liking their independence and their ability to contribute financially to the family. Already an estimated nineteen million women are in the workforce."

Phillips looks to another panel member. "Ms. Loeser, I believe that your organization has a transitioning program."

Herta Loeser takes the mike. "Yes, we work with companies to provide internships for women re-entering the labor force. The conditions of these internships makes them very similar to internships for students. They get experience to show on their resumes.

"I'd like to mention another concept that could be implemented by any organization that wants its jobs to appeal to young mothers," says Loeser. "I suggest providing what I call a change-of-pace job—change of pace from mothering—so the women don't use the same energies on the job that they do in caring for their children. That's important if you want to keep a mother on the job. If she does emotionally exhausting work, a young mother will become disillusioned because she faces another emotionally exhausting job at home.

"While caretaking jobs—working with disturbed people or with the elderly—are easy to find, a young mother would fare better in a somewhat neutral office job."

Felice Schwartz voices approval of Loeser's recommendations. "At Catalyst we favor that same kind of consideration for our employees who bear the emotional strain of child rearing. We advise our clients to let women who have babies decide when they feel psychologically and physically well enough to return, bonded with their babies and satisfied with the child care they've chosen.

"Like interning, we believe that women should return from maternity leave at less than full-time, if they wish, and provide them with help to get the work done when they're working part-time."

"Mr. Olmstead," says Phillips, "what do you say about this?"

A middle-aged, intense-sounding man, Olmstead responds, "I think that even after a child is a few months old, responsibilities of child rearing justify flexible scheduling, job-sharing for the mother *or* the father, or time off. Too many companies give employees the impression that taking time off for family is in a class with "calling in sick" when you're not sick. Making it possible for parents to show up at an all-important ball game or piano recital can give you more relaxed, productive, and satisfied employees—and a staff that is not riddled with vacant positions.

"Let a woman split a job with another person doing the same type of job," Olmstead advises. "Since part-time work tends to be low status and low paying, the alternative—two people of similar skills sharing one full-time job—is one way they can work limited hours while staying on at a well-paid level. This technique has been very popular for human-service jobs with a high burnout factor.

"But, I think any job is a good candidate for job sharing. If you can get a well-qualified employee by offering a job sharing arrangement, why not do it?"

Sophie Dermatis leans forward to the microphone. "Sometimes," she says, "you can get around the need for job sharing or other flexible arrangements by job enrichment—providing jobs that give women a chance to exercise their valued skills and letting them know that their contributions are appreciated.

"The reason that job enrichment works is that if you have a job where you're appreciated—and well-paid, too—somehow you juggle things without getting bitter. But women become frustrated when they're doing work they dislike, in jobs where there's no prospect of promotion, while at the same time feeling tied down at home."

Felice Schwartz interjects: "Businesses have a big opportunity with women who are not working. Not only does the female labor force represent opportunity, it's also a necessity. Because of a shortage in skilled labor, brought on by such factors as a lower birthrate in recent years, businesses must welcome females and their otherwise-scarce talent.

"But my aim," adds Schwartz, "is broader than just jobs for women. It is equal opportunity for women in the workplace, a goal now made achievable by worker demographics and civil rights laws. However, businesses that depend upon women to solve many of their staffing problems will have to start providing the goodies that many women have hoped for for years—everything from gender-blind job assignment policies, to freedom from sexual harassment, to assistance with child care and a guarantee that children will not impede their career advancement.

"Men and women in the corporate world will have to do something they feel uncomfortable doing," insists Schwartz, "and that is to talk honestly about how maternity affects a woman's capacity to work outside the home."

With a concluding tone in her voice and a glance at Phillips, Schwartz indicates the end of her talk.

Phillips thanks his participants. "You have made us realize that, these days, successful recruiting demands that companies recognize and support balance between work and family life. That can be done by the use of flex scheduling, part-time work, and company help with day care to assimilate many valuable women workers into the workplace."

The fifteen-page "Booklet of General Information about Job Sharing"—which includes a discussion of how to handle fringe benefits, types of jobs being shared, and a sample time chart—is available for $2.50 from New Ways to Work Publications, 149 Ninth St., San Francisco, California 94103.

Many women drop out of the workforce to raise children or to accommodate a husband's career. The way to lure them back is to simplify a transition back to part-time or full-time employment.

Start a day-care operation and accept anyone's children, thereby making the operation self-sufficient or even profitable.

Let a woman share a job with another person doing the same type of work. Since part-time work tends to be low status and low paying, the alternative—two people of similar skills sharing one full-time job— is one way they can work limited hours while staying on at a well-paid level.

Chapter 9

My Customer, My Employee

"**O**ur customers make some of our best employees." That was the headline on a "statement stuffer," an advertisement that one company enclosed with its monthly billings to customers. The company reprinted the ad in a larger format, placed copies in acrylic holders, and displayed them in reception areas and at checkout counters. A stack of job applications accompanied each display.

A dearth of job-hunting teenagers resulting from low birthrates in the late 1970s and early 1980s, coupled with a generally tight labor market, has prompted one well-known fast-food company to raise the age ceiling on its labor pool. The fast-food chain now seeks adults as well as teens to cook, clean, assist and manage its outlets.

Where is this company finding its new, mature workforce? "We recruit older workers from among our customers," says Stanley Stein, a senior vice president at the company.

Some companies like to hire customers to work for them because they think such employees will have a better appreciation for customer service. They also view customers as part of their candidate referral network. Customers and vendors who refer candidates are frequently rewarded with merchandise certificates or other favors for every referred job candidate who is hired and stays on the job for three months or more.

Prospective employees enter your place of business every day . . . disguised as customers. Here are a number of ways to reach them:

- Include a "want ad" flyer with every customer purchase.
- Create in-store poster displays.
- Have video, rear-projection television, or filmstrip display running on continuous loop at checkout counters—present a simple message using graphics and brief audio by a company spokesperson.
- Place a recruitment message in red ink on cash register receipts.
- Attach job notices to products.

Asked by management why they applied for work at one successful chain of pizza restaurants, employees offered main reasons: One was that they had been customers and liked the work atmosphere. The other reason was that their friends who worked there had encouraged them to apply. The employees also said they liked the flexible hours and teamwork style that made the job fun.

Another business used this message: "Place your name on our employment waiting list for great job opportunities." The employer didn't even have a waiting list. But once his message got out, he had a sudden need to create one.

J.C. Penney has sent statement stuffers to more than fifteen million of its credit customers. This method was quite successful, especially in building staff for seasonal employee demands, such as Christmas.

A small company can do the same thing.

Reach customers with employment messages in sack stuffers, in-store poster and video displays, cash register receipts, and job notices attached to products.

Send statement stuffers to credit customers, informing them of employment opportunities.

When you hire customers you are getting employees who are likely to be sensitive to customer needs and expectations.

CHAPTER 10

BECOME A LIGHT IN THE NIGHT

Roger Easton, President of General Electronics Trading and Manufacturing Company in Cincinnati, credits his company's low 15 percent annual turnover to the fact that his employees like working for General Electronics; and they tell their friends about their satisfaction.

He capitalizes upon that job satisfaction by paying employees for "suspects" who become prospects.

But, says Easton, General Electronics' employees play the role of voluntary recruiters, without inducement. They do it unwittingly, he says, whenever they compliment their employer in public.

Employee satisfaction is a valuable tool for any employer faced with a staffing challenge. There's only one way to acquire use of the tool—treat employees humanely and work with them to develop fulfilling job situations.

When employers demonstrate genuine concern for their employees' satisfaction with their work, they earn a bonus—superior performance. Employees work harder, their work quality is better, and they are less likely to leave.

When an employer's attitude toward employees is that the employees are being paid to do a job and that if they don't, they'll be fired, they know it "within forty-five minutes of taking a job," says Larry Wilson, training guru and management consultant.

"Right away," says Wilson, "they start doing whatever they must do to avoid being fired—usually no more than that."

Some of them take revenge on employers by intentionally sabotaging products or services—being rude to customers and neglecting them, for instance.

These are not problems that Roger Easton and his managers face. The president of the privately owned company summarized his strategies for enlisting his employees in an ongoing prospect–referral system.

About ten years ago the company instituted the work team concept, says Easton. It closely resembles "empowered work teams" that are popular today.

"Our people know that their managers listen to their ideas. And our managers know that listening to and implementing employee input is a primary job responsibility.

"A bonus system based upon profit shows employees that they have a stake in the company's performance. We all seem to want the same thing, prosperity for the company, so employees and managers cooperate, share, and help each other.

"It means a lot to General Electronics people that we don't have 'bosses,' in the old, authoritarian sense of the word. Our bosses are coaches. Mentors. They advise and suggest. Their role is no more or no less important than the job of an assembler or quality control inspector.

"The key to our success in recruiting is that our employees like working for us. They feel that they are doing their job-seeking friends a favor when they tell them about us. We have a reputation in the community as a good place to work. That reputation is worth a full-page employment ad every week in the newspaper."

An important part of Easton's calculated method of maintaining that reputation is his publicity program. The guiding philosophy of the program is: "Do something for the community that you really want to do. Then make sure, through publicity, that everyone knows about it."

The company follows the basic public relations principle of publicizing only action—of *doing* something that is beneficial to the interests of one's audience (customers, prospective employers, suppliers, government) and *then* announcing it. In other words: *Make* news and then announce it.

General Electronics' advertising and public relations manager disseminates news releases in appropriate form (feature article, column item, radio script, captioned slide for television news, and so on) *only* when he is sure that the media will want to use it. There is no publicity schedule to keep.

A release was distributed (and it was followed up by phone calls to key media contacts) when a warming house that General Electronics built at an ice rink in a city park was to be dedicated. The mayor attended the dedication. Photographers snapped him pulling a cord that released a curtain covering the plaque.

A half-sheet not clipped to the news release announced the photo opportunity.

I've summarized some of the most important publicity tips for small business that I gathered in a conversation with Ron Yonikawa, General Electronics' advertising and public relations manager.

Avoid giving the impression to the media that you *expect* your publicity to be used. The barriers erected by most editors against public-relations-generated publicity, are weakened by the perception that your approach is *helpful*, not demanding, and that you will not be indignant at rejection.

Instead of sending cluster-bombing releases to every medium that has an address, send the media only material on topics they frequently use, in formats that they prefer, at the times they want it, and addressed to the staff member responsible for processing your kind of material.

Selecting topics with universal human appeal that automatically grasp the attention of editors and readers is the single most vital step in a publicity process, Yonikawa said.

Be aware at all times that every member of an audience, no matter how obscure his or her specialization nor how sober his or her demeanor, is a human being with a normal complement of human feelings and reactions. Information should be written like human interest stories.

Avoid mundane, unchanging publicity practices. For instance, do not time after time present the media with completed articles on news release letterhead that implies that the sponsor would resent the editor's pencil. Offer article ideas, fact sheets, background information, and opportunity to order articles and to specify the articles' features and content. This way you involve editors and writers and demonstrate respect for their professional abilities.

Instead of *news release* use the term *editorial fact sheet*. Write the fact sheet like an article. It takes only seconds for media professionals to realize their good luck—the fact sheet is a well-written article. Meanwhile, they do not feel "used."

A related approach is presenting oneself as a freelance writer, thereby concealing "propaganda" intent. This tactic neutralizes editors' distrust of publicity and public relations material that they commonly consider questionable in quality and accuracy.

Or, persuade other freelancers to do a story. This approach saves time and money that a company would spend doing the work itself, and utilizes the freelancers' existing contacts.

Posted on a bulletin board just outside the door to the advertising and public relations department is a memo from Easton distributed several years ago to supervisors and managers. He wrote: "We want to influence customers to buy from us, and we want to persuade people to apply for work here, so we do *not* hide our light under a basket. We tap into the old grapevine by which important information is communicated in this community, and we keep that grapevine well-fed with nutrients that the grapevine absorbs and transmits."

If General Electronics and Manufacturing Company has a staffing problem, the problem is not difficulty in finding applicants. The problem—more correctly a brief and welcome dilemma—is in choosing an applicant from among several who are qualified for a position.

When you treat people like people they work harder, they do better work, and they're less likely to leave.

Bosses should function as coaches and mentors. They should listen and advise.

Maintain a referral system that pays employees for nominating frontline prospects.

Chapter 11

The School Connection

Some small businesses may be able to learn from large corporations that maintain liaison programs with job candidates while they are still attending school.

Megasys Corporation "adopts" juniors and seniors at local high schools to work in company internship programs. They call it their Adopt-a-School program. One of the company's intern programs is with California State University Fullerton. Students learn computer programming and help with marketing. Megasys pays them and they earn college credit.

"In the future we will see college and high school students targeted by companies early in their academic careers. They will be offered educational benefits, skills training, and job enrichment in exchange for accepting a job," says Stephen F. Guinn, director of executive development at Pittsburg-based PSP: Human Resource Development, a company which provides organizational psychology services to businesses.

Contact the high schools in your community to suggest adopting juniors and seniors to join an internship program at your firm.

One newspaper had trouble finding qualified entry-level electricians, especially minority candidates. They developed a junior college apprenticeship program to help solve this problem. Both the newspaper management and the student apprentices had the opportunity for close inspection of each other. This frequently sets the stage for job offers prior to student graduation.

Small business can learn from watching the Eastman Kodak Company. Through its Kodak Scholars Program, the company provides grants to top students at thirty-five colleges. Kodak scholars—50 percent of whom are members of minority groups—receive full tuition support for sophomore year through graduation, plus stipends for three years of graduate study. The program also provides one summer of employment with Eastman Kodak.

"The purpose is to link up Eastman Kodak with the best students in areas of study related to our business," explains Stanley C. Wright, director of corporate contributions for Kodak. "We want to hire those students on graduation."

To strengthen the scholarship program, Kodak added a mentor program. Its mission is to familiarize students with Kodak and to build loyalty.

"You can't simply throw money at top students, though," says Wright. "You have to add certain ingredients to make it work. For example, our various operating companies get involved early and students' summer jobs with the company relate to their fields of study."

Burger King Corporation's Crew Education Assistance Program offers scholarships to hourly employees. Qualified workers can obtain up to two thousand dollars to attend any licensed, accredited college or vocational–technical institution. To be eligible, employees must first work an average of fifteen hours per week for three months, and they must maintain a C grade average or better. The program awards an additional thousand dollars to one hundred employees with a B average.

Waiting for people to graduate before approaching them is the old-fashioned way. Don't wait—contact students while they're still in school. Visit high school campuses, local colleges and universities, and vocational and technical schools. All over the country, businesses are reaching out to younger students to begin building early interest in specific jobs. Some organizations even approach grade-schoolers with invitations to tour their facilities.

Notes PSP's Guinn: "Companies must sell themselves to prospective employees. A growing number of candidates want to know what you have to offer and how you are going to match their ambitions and meet their needs.

"Extra effort at recruiting is needed because of a shortage of qualified people to hire. It's also necessary in order to help students *become* qualified."

There is a growing mismatch between the skills needed in the workplace and the skills workers possess.

The Motorola Company, New York Telephone Company, and other major employers report that eighty percent of job applicants can't pass basic-level English comprehension or math tests. Applicants for jobs with independent companies are generally believed to be even less qualified.

"The 'skills gap' is a problem that's no longer confined to large companies," says Robert Martin, vice president and executive director of the Center for Work Force Preparation and Quality Education of the U.S. Chamber of Commerce. The Center is the Chamber's major initiative to help businesses deal with problems stemming from poorly educated and poorly trained workers. It was established to help reform and reshape the U.S. educational system.

Small-business owners complain that many of today's young, entry-level workers are unprepared for work. Many of these employees run up high absentee rates, fail to do high-quality work, and lack a cooperative work attitude. One solution is to do what the big companies do: Establish connections with students and develop their commitment to your company before they graduate.

Adapt big-company recruitment ideas to your small company.

Organize an internship program for students at local high schools and colleges.

Establish connections with students and develop their commitment to your company before they graduate.

Free Booklet: To help companies manage scholarship programs, the Council for Aid to Education—51 Madison Ave., Suite 2200, New York, New York 10010; 212-689-2400—has produced a free booklet: *Guidelines: How to Develop and Administer a Corporate Scholarship Program.*

Chapter 12

Indirect Recruiting: Offer Education

Obtaining an education is an important goal for people today. Linking work with education may be the key to limiting turnover in service and production industries. Giving people who are still in school the opportunity to get "experiential education" as part-time interns is a way to find good employees.

Interning is one of many ways to use the lure of education and self-improvement to attract employees. In our so-called knowledge economy, where success is achieved with personal knowledge and skills, education is an effective recruiting strategy.

One way to find interns is to talk with the placement directors at trade and technical schools, and at colleges and universities. You can also call high school counselors or college professors and ask them to recommend interns.

Hire a person to work as an intern for a couple of hours per day, or full-time for thirteen weeks during summer vacation. Always assign the intern a specific project. Clearly state objectives, recommend how to do the work, and make sure that the intern has the tools and the resources needed to do the job. If you set interns adrift upon a sea of uncertainties, you will risk losing their interest and enthusiasm. Worst of all, you'll lose the possibility of hiring them after graduation.

At the end of the intern period, meet with the intern to share thoughts about possible employment with your organization. If there is mutual interest, take the steps necessary to bring the person onboard.

Another way to find an optimal employee is through an education incentive program.

Herb Schervish, owner and operator of two large-volume Burger King stores in the Detroit, Michigan, area, launched an education incentive program. Schervish financed an eight-month exploratory study to measure the effect of his program on turnover and productivity. He found that, for employees taking advantage of the program, turnover rate dropped from 179 percent to 38.7 percent. Turnover rate is calculated as follows: Subtract the total number of employees at the end of the current year from the total number of employees at the end of the previous year. Divide the difference (either positive or negative) by the number of W2 forms filled out during the current year. The result is your *turnover rate*.

A grocery store chain in Michigan had a turnover rate of about 300 percent. Although management couldn't pinpoint the problem, it understood that turnover was a *symptom,* not a *cause* of the problem. The Winninger

Institute, headed by Tom Winninger, conducted a management training program for the chain.

Its first discovery was that management was *not* the problem. They later discovered the real problem: The inability to create an educational environment for new hires. New employees weren't trained for jobs assigned to them. They were just put in the aisles to stock shelves with no more than vague, general instructions. Consequently, their performance was poor, and their self-esteem suffered. To these employees, "upward mobility" was a meaningless term. Because they felt they had a *job*, not a *career*, they were constantly scouting out new jobs. Or they would simply quit.

One way to attract the *right* employee to the *right* job is to run a local media ad offering a free training seminar in the hopes of attracting employment "prospects." Seminar topics should address the business of the sponsoring company—a flower shop might put on a seminar about uses of dried flowers; a hardware store might sponsor a demonstration of techniques for home improvement; a garden store could present landscaping ideas.

At the end of the presentation, distribute "nomination forms" or flyers pitching career opportunities at *your* company and ask for the names and contact information of possible employment prospects.

Some employers start their own trade schools. During their classes, real-life company situations are examined. At the end employment opportunities and interviews are offered to anyone interested in a career with their organization, and flyers are distributed.

Less extreme than founding your own trade school is to co-sponsor and teach some classes at a local vocational or technical school. Media ads and posters in stores are effective methods of advertising courses. Sometimes a local cable television or radio station will advertise a business in exchange for a public service announcement submitted by the business.

Job fairs still are common and effective. According to The Food Marketing Institute (FMI), an association of supermarket operators and grocery wholesalers in Washington, D.C., at least 45 percent of the companies in its industry still recruit through job fairs.

Obtaining an education is an important goal for people today. Linking work with education may be the key to limiting turnover in service and production industries.

Always assign a new intern to a specific project. Clearly state objectives, recommend how to do the work, and make sure that the intern has the tools and resources to do the job.

Education is an effective recruiting strategy in our "knowledge economy." Success is achieved with skills and qualifications.

Chapter 13

Play Your Network

You belong to many networks. A network is a chain of people linked together by a professional or personal interest. Networks can be as simple as your group of friends at the Chamber of Commerce, or at the Lions or Kiwanis clubs. The network might consist of members of a professional group, such as a sales and marketing club, members of your church or synagogue, or the guys at the hunting club.

A network can also be as extensive as a nationwide computer hook-up or all the members of a national trade association.

Mention to the members of your networks, including all the customers you talk to during the week, that you are hiring. Then sit back and let the network spread the message, sending applicants to your door.

A more formal approach was tried by fast-growing CPS Employment Services Network of Westchester, Illinois. The company combined an ad with an open house. Sixty people who attended the open house were asked for names of others who might be interested in the company. The sixty prospects at the open house were led through a casual yet structured introduction to the company. Each attendee watched a video, filled out a short application form, and was screened by a manager.

You can expand your network by registering with these services:

- Jobtrak (800-999-8725). When you call this computer network with your part-time, temporary, or full-time job listing, it will be posted at 130 or more college career centers for two weeks. Most colleges linked to Jobtrak are on the West Coast, but the network is expanding to other parts of the country. The cost is $12.50 for the first college listing and $7.50 for each college after that.
- Operation Transition (703-614-5322). Managed by the U.S. Army, this service provides prospective employers with both a referral system and a job-posting service that puts them in contact with people leaving the armed services in search of another career.
- InternAmerica (800-456-7335). Operated by Ford and Ford Careerworks, in Needham, Massachusetts.

Networking is high-impact, low-cost recruiting. Try it.

Ask employees to spread the word that you are hiring.

Put on an open house for potential employees at your store or plant.

Chapter 14

Flex Your Schedule to Lure Employees

Roger Q. Carlin is an aspiring novelist who makes ends meet by writing publicity for a local temporary-help firm.

He wakes up at 6:30 in the morning and works at his own writing projects until noon. Then, after lunch, he goes to the Porpoise Temporary Help service to work for about four hours. That earns him enough to pay his bills yet keep his dream alive.

Mabel Struthers and Ann Pieper have known each other since high school. They still live in the same neighborhood, just a block apart.

One evening they were talking on the phone about how hard it is to get the kids off to school before leaving for work, and how much they'd like to be home when their children return from school. Later that same evening, Ann heard the subject of "job sharing" discussed on the radio. She called her friend to tell her about it. They decided that they would develop a job-sharing plan to propose to Mabel's employer. The idea was that, one week, Ann would work mornings and Mabel would work afternoons. They would switch mornings and afternoons the next week, and continue with that flip-flop schedule week after week. That way, everyday, each of them would be present for either their children's departure or return from school.

Mabel's employer, Carl Terry, said: "As long as the work gets done, I don't care who works how much or when."

Phil had retired as a mail carrier last fall. At first he loved not setting the alarm clock; he enjoyed doing chores around the house on his own time. But he soon realized that he missed working. Phil started reading the want ads and, in a couple of days, found one that caught his interest: "Help Wanted: Retired. Part-time mail room clerk. Work afternoons, four days a week."

Phil got the job and is now much happier.

Homemakers, single mothers, the retired and semi-retired, the self-employed, and others who prefer part-time or flexible hours as a lifestyle, constitute a large and growing "contingent workforce." One startling estimate is that between twenty-nine million and thirty-six million Americans—ranging from on-call nurses and lunch-hour cashiers to short-term aerospace engineers—were contingent workers in 1988. This is according to Richard Belous of the National Planning Association. The figure is said to be increasing steadily.

In a national study conducted by the Families and Work Institute of New York City and reported in the *Los Angeles Times* in March 1992, 70 percent of the companies surveyed said they offer their employees personal leaves of absence; nearly 48 percent permit job sharing, and about 22 percent offer both maternity and paternity leaves.

Faced with ever-lengthening commutes and increasing "family time" demands for single-parent and dual working-spouse households, a growing number of American workers are seeking alternatives to their traditional nine-to-five jobs.

Among the alternatives are part-time work, compressed work weeks, job sharing, telecommuting, and unpaid personal leaves of absence. Business is showing interest in many of these areas.

Such creative job-force scheduling tends to be inspired by labor shortages, air-quality regulations, and productivity enhancing campaigns. But, increasingly, managers recognize that making concessions for an employee's family obligations is not a sign of permissiveness or unnecessary coddling. It is a good way to help recruit and retain valuable workers.

I recommend contingent workforce strategies because they provide a resource for top-notch talent. I've used flex scheduling in my own business for years, and credit it with improving productivity and work quality.

Some employers find that more flexible policies, such as voluntary unpaid leaves, reduces hiring costs and the expense of training new workers.

Some employees are motivated toward alternative schedules by this kind of thinking: "Why should you give up your life for your job if the employer gives up on you when you're fifty?" So said Bonnie Michaels, president of Managing Work and Family, an Evanston, Illinois, consulting group. "Employees are increasingly looking for a better balance between work and home."

When people are allowed to work *when* they want and *as much* as they want, they are more likely to enjoy their work and to be productive. Some people want or need flexibility in their hours, due to circumstances beyond their control. Others like being "their own bosses," working when and where they wish. And there are those who simply are not interested in a career climb, so full-time commitment is not important.

Often these employees are working to sustain an expense, such as college tuition, the cost of private music lessons, or extended medical care for a loved one. Because they are pursuing a valuable objective, they are usually steady, motivated workers.

Many employers have found that time flexibility, far from disrupting operations, actually improves both morale and employee retention. It also increases productivity, and decreases turnover, tardiness, and absenteeism.

When you publicly offer flexible hours, that one move reaches a large number of prospects in your community who wouldn't otherwise consider your jobs.

The energy of employees who work only part-time is released during a shorter period. The result in terms of productivity is comparable to that of releasing a stretched rubber band ("energy packing").

Russ Cunningham, fifty-seven, vice president for human resources at Pacific Gas and Electric in San Francisco, approved a job-sharing arrangement for two mothers, each of whom works three days a week. "I think we're getting more out of them now," said Cunningham. "During their days off, each calls in to the office to check on how things are going. So we not only get the three days a week that we're paying for, but we also get some of their at-home time."

Part-time employees generally do *not* have part-time commitment, as some employers fear.

It's common for flexible hours to increase productivity, which is one way of saying that a flexible-hours policy reduces an organization's compensation costs. Productivity often increases because the incidence of burnout decreases.

That was the finding of Deere Credit Corporation, which serves employees of equipment manufacturer Deere and Company. Deere and Company offers flextime—employees may work any eight hours they choose between seven a.m. and six p.m. as long as they make arrangements with their managers.

Burnout has been called a "malaise of the spirit." An employee who once was a prime contributor no longer seems to get excited about his job. A formerly cooperative employee becomes inflexible and difficult to get along with. A once-reliable employee now often calls in sick. Burned-out employees are easily fatigued, bored with their work, quick to anger, cynical, hostile and apathetic, and they have a difficult time recognizing the problems and concerns of others. They withdraw. They become rigid and inflexible. And they're ineffective and inefficient in their work. Eventually it becomes harder and harder for them to think clearly, to make decisions, or to accomplish even routine tasks.

You may be able to prevent these problems by offering flexible hours.

Contingent workers might solve all your staffing problems. Are you pursuing this source of employees assertively? Shout your welcome to anyone who wants to work hours that don't jibe with the standard nine-to-five, five-days-a-week work schedule. "What's your pleasure?" could be your message to your school connections, to your network contacts, to your present employees, to women, and to customers who are potential employees.

Make yourself receptive to contingency workers by adjusting your schedule to their needs.

"Businesses that resist the trend to more flexible hours could be at a disadvantage in future recruiting," says Barbara Sanfilippo, the author, speaker, and consultant for the firm of Romano & Sanfilippo that specializes in quality services and sales culture.

Mothers

Many mothers who hesitate to work because their children attend school will work if you allow them to work between the time their children leave for school and the time they return.

You might receive an enthusiastic response if you announce that you will be willing to work with two or more people on a job-sharing arrangement. It's a great way for a woman to re-enter the workforce. Job-sharing employees share one salary, benefits and responsibilities. Participants are responsible for calling their partner if they are sick, plan to be out of town, or simply don't feel like working.

Formal job-share programs are offered by about 16 percent of U.S. companies, says the American Society for

Personnel Administration. Several state governments also offer job sharing. In Massachusetts, more than two hundred pairs of job sharers hold civil service positions.

"Personal needs have changed," says Nicole Payne, manager of the alternative work options program for the Commonwealth of Massachusetts. "But, unfortunately, people in power have lagged behind employee needs in both the private and the public sectors."

From the employer's point of view, job "partnering" (sharing) is a way to get full-time work from part-time employees.

Sanfilippo reports: "One top loan producer I know was having a baby and wanted to job-share for a year. Her manager wasn't crazy about the idea. But results were very positive. Instead of one stressed-out employee, the manager had two effective employees."

Among the various job-share partners at Levi Strauss are Helen Purdum and Barbara O'Connell. Helen works all day Monday, Tuesday, and Thursday, while Barbara works daily from seven a.m. to two p.m. They are paid as part-timers, depending on how many hours they work. Their twenty-hour weeks qualify them for health, life insurance and pension benefits. Vacation is prorated. (Hiring two people to do one job does cost an employer a bit more than having one person in that position.)

Like most job-share partners, Purdum and O'Connell communicate constantly. They meet when both are in the office and communicate with notes and phone calls.

What are the trade-offs? A slimmer paycheck for each, less control over the job, slower advancement and, so Purdum points out, "Sometimes decision making has to go on without me."

THE RETIRED

About 48 percent of retired people surveyed by the American Association of Retired Persons (AARP), the nation's largest organization of people fifty and older, said that they would return to work if they found the right job opportunity.

Labor statisticians predict that the fifty-five-and-over group will grow at a rate of 0.4 percent to 1.2 percent until the year 2000. People are living longer and staying healthier than ever. As a result, older people are unwilling to limit themselves to traditional retirement pursuits, such as golf, fishing, and grandchildren, or to endless days of rocking chairs and petunia potting. They need work to keep boredom at bay.

A good reason for *not* hiring older people is hard to find. Statistics show that they are more reliable than young people: They call in sick less often, and aren't as apt to be distracted by child-care responsibility, socializing, or other activities demanded by youth.

Charles McIntyre, manager of the Stebbins-Anderson home center store in Baltimore, Maryland, says: "Older workers in this business are very service-oriented. They don't feel that it's demeaning to be polite, or to rush to a customer's aid. That's not necessarily the lifestyle of younger people. I don't want to put them down; it's just that the older people grew up in a different time."

But, to convince older people to work for you, you must first convince them that you understand their needs and interests—their motivations.

To contact older prospects, ask your company's retirees and former employees to suggest candidates. Once a year, the Travelers Insurance Company invites all their retired employees to an "unretirement" party, where they try to lure their retirees back to full- or part-time work.

Some companies seek to retain their valuable older employees by offering them part-time work when they are about to retire. My own father, well past retirement, continues to be active in his real estate consulting firm. Seniors bring a wealth of experience, stability and loyalty to an organization. Many have customer-service savvy that the younger generation lacks. And with Social Security guidelines prohibiting full-time work, seniors make excellent candidates for flex scheduling.

Do you recall the recent TV ad showing a friendly looking, grandfatherly man on his way to an early-morning job at McDonalds'? He was pictured as capable and endearing, able to show the younger employees a thing or two. The ad solicited job applications from older workers.

Another prominent food service company, Kentucky Fried Chicken, displays its respect for the older generation through the "Colonel's Tradition" program. The fact that the company was founded by an elderly man in a white suit known to millions as "The Colonel" is advertised proudly.

Once a company commits itself to flex scheduling and hires a number of people to work flexible hours, the company will find that it can rapidly adjust the strength of its labor force in response to seasonal or market demands. They can staff up or staff down accordingly, without routinely hiring and firing. Flexibility in accommodating employees' scheduling needs is also an excellent retention tool.

In many cases, part-time employees grow into valuable full-time associates, especially when they are given the same training and opportunity as full-time workers. On the other hand, if they prefer to continue working reduced hours, older-aged employees often remain steady, loyal, and dedicated workers—rock-solid assets to your company—for years to come.

Arlene Falk Withers, senior vice president and human relations officer at Transamerica Life Companies in Los Angeles, California, says: "Companies that get past the old notions of management and direct supervision, and embrace flexible scheduling and employee empowerment to get the work done, are going to have the competitive edge in the next century."

Business is interested in part-time staffing, job sharing, flex-time, compressed work week, and telecommuting. I recommend using "contingent" workforces because they provide a resource for top-notch talent.

Part-time employees generally do *not* have part-time commitment, as some employers fear. It's common for flexible hours to increase productivity, which is one way of saying that a flexible-hours policy reduces an organization's compensation costs.

Flexible policies, such as voluntary unpaid leaves, can reduce labor costs and the expense of training new workers.

Chapter 15

Brochures for the VCR

If you're in business, you've got to have a brochure, right? In the minds of most business people, you don't even exist if you don't have a brochure.

Brochures are indeed important. They can help you save time by prequalifying applicants for jobs. However, with the sudden and revolutionary advent of the computer age, the concept of "brochure" needs radical updating.

Johnny can't read. But he sure can play Nintendo. Video is "in." Computers are "in." The youngest generation of employees is computer literate. As an employer seeking to attract potential employees from that new labor pool, you *must* utilize methods that are now the most common part of their daily lives. Here are three ways to go:

Video Brochure. A company in Maine produced a contemporary music video, which it showed at job fairs and high school recruiting sessions. You can screen a video brochure at:

- Career seminars, on-site recruiting sessions, and job fairs. A video is likely to attract more people than a person speaking at a booth.
- Meetings of Distributive Education Clubs of America (DECA) and other job development programs. DECA conducts nationwide business programs for the education of high school students.
- Your place of business. Set up a monitor near cash registers or the front door, where the video can play on a continuous loop all day.

Computer Diskette Brochure. Hire a company that produces software programs to create a "brochure" on computer diskette. Be sure that the company you choose has experience in computer graphics. (Consult your local phone directory, or the directory for the nearest large city. Check under "Computers: Software and Services.")

Distribute your diskette by offering it in employment ads and through your other brochure formats. Make it available at career seminars and job fairs. Give it to your prospects.

Print Brochure. The tried-and-true print brochure is useful in its own special way. Prospects can review them more easily than they can video or computer versions. However, if you do choose to stick with print brochures, you should fill them with color and graphics, such as photos and drawings, to make them more appealing to the TV/computer generation. The Quick-Trip Corporation uses a tri-fold, four-color brochure that incorporates a nomination form on the back page. The brochure describes the advantages of a career with Quick-Trip and sketches possible career paths.

Offer brochures in acrylic point-of-purchase displays, put them in shopping bags, mail them to a list of prospects purchased from a direct mail company, attach them to certain products, or distribute them as newspaper inserts. You can also promote the print version in your video and computer diskette versions.

Buy mailing lists that have been customized specifically for *your* relevant demographic parameters. Many mailing list brokers exist, but one of the largest is Dunhill Mailing Lists in New York City (800-223-5464). Dunhill supplies almost every kind of mailing list conceivable. For instance, you can order a list of all the females in an age group who live in a certain state or zip-code area, and who subscribe to *Women In Business* magazine. Looking for a good mechanic? Buy a list of *Popular Mechanics* subscribers, or people who belong to vintage-automobile clubs.

VIDEO PRODUCTION

Ask the media departments at local universities or community colleges to let their students produce your video for credit. As an inducement for the school to cooperate, offer to donate a copy of the video brochure for use in the school's career placement program.

If a cooperative venture with students doesn't work out, look for a reliable production company. Carefully consider smaller companies that charge less. Big production companies sometimes charge much more, yet don't always give you a higher-quality product.

Another option is to rent the facilities of your local public access cable channel, if available, to produce your own.

Once the program has been produced, copies of your "video brochure" can be made at a reasonable cost. 110-minute videocassettes (called "dubs") will cost about $320. This includes the cost of the cassettes, label face and spine, plus cardboard sleeve.

You may wish to hire a professional writer to pen the script for your video. If so, you can save time and money by first providing the writer with a list of points that you want to make in the video. These points are your answers to the question: "What can I say to convince a qualified applicant to work for me?"

Make sure the video portrays you and your business realistically, not with phony, slick images. You want your prospects to see the *real* story. Otherwise, after they become your employees, they may become disillusioned and leave.

Brochure Content

Design your video, computer, or print "brochure" to reach people you want to attract as employees. Do it with music, graphics, setting/environment, and the personalities of the actors that you choose for the video. Hire performers whose age and appearance represent the kind of employees you want to hire. If you're trying to recruit young adults, then young adults should appear in the video. If your goal is to hire retirees, then older people should play the parts.

An effective print brochure should include a "nomination form" (perhaps on the back cover), and six, eight or ten reasons why working for your company is a good opportunity.

Also include in the copy:

- Description of the company and its business. Brief history of your firm. Mission statement of twenty-five words or less.
- Opportunities for new employees. Mention benefits, but emphasize "opportunities."
- Basic qualifications required of employees.
- Quotes from named employees saying that your company is a fine place to work.
- Toll-free job line for applicants.

When a prospect views or reads your brochure, he or she should derive this message from it: "What you learn here on the ground floor will create the opportunity for you to become department manager, assistant store manager, and store manager. While you learn, you will be preparing for a career."

Don't refer to part-time work. Nobody considers working part-time to be preparation for a career or for promotion and raises. The food industry, for example, regularly refers to part-time work in its recruitment materials. As a direct result, a shortage of career-oriented people exists in that industry.

People shouldn't be offered "part-time work at a grocery store." They should be offered "an entry-level position in the food industry."

Disney teaches that all of its employees begin at entry-level. The company's philosophy holds that starting at the bottom is the way you get to the top.

Tell new employees specifically what they will learn and how it will affect future opportunity. Workers are motivated by the *dollar value* of training and by the opportunity to acquire knowledge and skills. Include in your brochure information about your value package (benefits), flexible scheduling, team culture, and opportunity for advancement. Not only will you dramatically improve your recruitment rate, but you'll also improve your retention rate.

The best brochures—those that are complete and accurate in *any* format—induce Mr. and Ms. Right to call, and Mr. and Ms. Wrong to keep looking.

Qualified people will "connect" with your company because they will see in the brochure that your organization meets their needs. Unqualified people will conclude that your organization is *not* for them. The result will be a savings in recruitment time and money.

The great value of a good brochure is that it induces Mr. and Ms. Right to call, and Mr. and Ms. Wrong to keep looking.

Contact media departments at local universities or community colleges. Ask them to let their students produce your video for credit.

Save time and money by supplying your video scriptwriter with a list of points that you want to make in the script.

CHAPTER 16

ADVERTISING ALTERNATIVE: MARKETING

Advertising has its place, and so do public relations and promotional activity. But when you want to add qualified people to your staff, think *marketing,* not just advertising.

Advertising is a limiting concept. Marketing, on the other hand, incorporates all communications that influence people to make buying decisions. In this case, we're referring to the decision to take a job in your organization.

My friend, Moriah, is an account supervisor in a local ad agency. "Businesses waste money on employment advertising," she says. "They advertise in the wrong media, like the newspaper's classified ad section. That's a very general audience. Instead, they ought to advertise in specialized media that reach the people they want to hire."

Moriah is right. If your audience is young people, consider advertising on rock-and-roll and other pop music radio stations, as well as in high school and college newspapers or yearbooks. Even if *you* don't care for rock 'n' roll, your prospects may be mesmerized by it.

On the other hand, if it is mostly older people who possess the qualifications that you want in an employee, then you must accommodate that audience. Advertise in the publications put out by groups such as SCORE (Senior Corps of Retired Executives), Golden Age Clubs, local chapters of the American Association of Retired Persons, health and wellness programs, Goodwill agencies, and home extension services. In daily newspapers, you may be better off with display ads in the sections read by the kind of people you're trying to reach. Consider advertising in the food section or on the women's page; try the TV section, the handyman's weekly page, the outdoors section, or even the sports pages.

In terms of an ad's content, it should answer the question that every prospect asks: "What's in it for me?" Immediately after the ad's heading, list benefits that will interest people reading about the job for the first time. Write about something unique in your business, something that's likely to stir a response. You know what these messages are because your present employees are influenced by them.

Avoid generalities, such as: "Company seeks individual with broad background in accounting." You'll end up with resumes from every Tom, Dick, and Mary who ever balanced a bank statement. Instead, use snappy, specific, hard-hitting, emotionally appealing words and headlines to grab attention: "Top dollar paid for experienced kitchen help," or "Excellent benefits for qualified front-desk manager."

Kentucky Fried Chicken once ran an ad campaign to attract applicants for managerial jobs. Using the company logo, the ad drew a minimal response. KFC was tempted to give up on newspaper advertising altogether. But they decided to give it one more try. This time, their ad omitted the logo and only used copy that focused on the benefits of the job and the redeeming features of KFC. The turnaround in response rate was dramatic; an increase from two or three responses per ad, to 40–60 responses.

In writing your ad copy, be sure not to make wild claims about the benefits of working for your company. People are pretty good at recognizing statements that sound too good to be true.

If you feel that you must advertise in a newspaper's classified ad section, make sure that your ad stands out. Box it. Use large display type. Use color or graphics, such as a photo.

The better your company's reputation, the better the response will be to your employment advertising. The first thing to do when you set out to build a reputation as a good employer is to *be* a good employer. Do something beneficial for your employees; help community organizations with money, donated labor, or donated expertise. People find out about these activities one way or another, and they'll apply for your jobs before they answer your competitor's ads. You can then call a newspaper editor, or send out a one-page press release about what you've done. When you can get a newspaper or other medium to run a positive story about you, you've got an advantage over advertising. News and feature stories simply are more believable. People know that you paid for advertising, but they believe that the newspaper mentioned you because it was legitimate news.

Publicity helps generate a positive image that is a powerful attraction for qualified job prospects. Various communication methods reinforce each other. Advertising, publicity, promotional activities, direct marketing such as mailing and telemarketing, and public relations action all make contributions to a strong marketing message.

People who read ads are looking for a job. But when you want a well-qualified employee, you are looking for a person who isn't looking for a job. The person is happy and productive where he or she is. When you find such people, try to persuade them that they would be even happier working for you. To successfully persuade a person who's employed to quit and to come to work for you, your marketing messages must all be concise, clear, and honest.

Advertising must be placed in media that reach people qualified for your job—people with interests and eligibility that match your business. This is called *focused advertising*. It makes more sense to spend $500 on an ad in an industry-specific or special-interest magazine if it attracts five qualified applicants than it does to spend $500 for classified ads in the local newspaper and receive resumes from fifteen or twenty unqualified people. To reach the exact kind of people you want, advertise in those publications tailored to the service or product that your company offers, whether it be parenting, food, health and beauty, home care, women's issues, working parents, or some other area. To reach seniors, target magazines geared toward groups concerned with financial investments. Advertise in media that serve specific hobbies related to your product or service.

Coupons are an effective advertising recruitment tool. People without resumes can conveniently fill out coupons that appear in your print advertising and mail them to you. You can also try trailers in your regular merchandise or service advertising. Just a box in the corner noting that jobs are available will do the job. Movie commercials work well. One supermarket I know achieves great results from run-ning film commercials on the big screen at the local movie theater.

Additional channels to consider are neighborhood newspapers, church bulletins, newsletters and PTA periodicals. Although their circulation may be low, the number of real job prospects in their readerships is high. The idea is to seek out media that produce the most qualified applicants at the lowest cost.

No matter where you put your advertising, work hard on the copy. Make sure that it reflects the needs and interests of your target audience. For example, when you want to lure part-time weekend counter help, don't offer retirement plans or investment programs. The ad should appeal to high school or college students by promoting flexible hours, advancement opportunity, and an hourly bonus for night and weekend work.

It's a basic rule in employment advertising to give prospective employees as much information as you can as early in your ads as you can. This reduces the number of unsuitable applicants.

Some prospects work at other jobs during regular business hours. To make it easier for them to call you, list varying hours to accommodate a variety of schedules. For example, instead of having applicants call between 2:00 and 4:00 p.m. Mondays through Fridays, request calls between 5:00 and 7:00 p.m. on Monday and Tuesday, and then from 10:00 a.m. until noon on Saturday.

We talked about setting up a special twenty-four-hour jobs hotline on voice mail and displaying that phone number in your ads. One of the voice mail options could be the personal line of the business owner or manager. But the first option would be the phone extension of an assistant. This person would ask pre-qualifying questions and schedule interviews.

You may wish to set up an answering machine message that changes as employment advertising changes. This way, potential applicants can call at their convenience, not just during the regular office hours that are at *your* convenience. Another option is for you to take calls in person for the first few days after an ad runs.

Publicity helps to generate a positive image of your company. That is a powerful attraction for qualified job prospects.

In reaching exactly the kind of people you want, advertise in "special interest" publications that relate to the service or product your company offers.

Don't just offer a job. Promote your company's merits and its *reputation* as an employer.

CHAPTER 17

CREATIVITY WITH TARGETED MAILING LISTS

A young sales manager, LeRoy Spurrier, stepped out of his office and walked down the corridor to the coffee room, where he ran into his friend, Serena. He leaned close to her and spoke in a conspiratorial tone. "Serena. Guess what? Remember the card that I tore off that mailer and sent back to Right Way Manufacturing about a job? They called. They want me to bring in a resume."

"Congratulations," said Serena, a small twinge of envy in her voice. "You going to do it?"

"Sure," said LeRoy. "Why not? They're a bigger company and I'll bet they pay better, too. Besides, it's closer to home."

Esther Connelly, president of Right Way Manufacturing Company, a snowmobile manufacturer in Grand Junction,

Minnesota, is sitting in the office of her company's operations manager, Johnny St. James, who's recently been doubling as human resources manager. "Johnny," said Esther, "since you're going to be doing our recruiting, let me tell you what we've been doing lately that really seems to work. We've had good luck this year with direct-mail recruiting. We've been buying mailing lists of people likely to qualify for our jobs, demographically. Then we mail them a flyer with a tear-off, postpaid card that they return to request more information." St. James leans forward, interested.

Connelly continues: "Usually we just mail to company addresses. It's amazing how these flyers are passed around to employees. When a person wants a different job, everybody else seems to know it." Connelly explains that the direct-mail approach is part of a strategy of "intrusive recruiting." This means going out and getting people who want a different job before they actually begin applying and sending out resumes.

"Besides mailing flyers, we do 'tele-recruiting,'" says Connelly. "We call people on carefully selected lists, tell them a little about the company, and ask them to come in and fill out an application. A list of competitors and suppliers worked well for us. We sent them the flyer with the tear-off card. I expect that association directories and membership lists for professional organizations—ready-made mailing lists—would work for us, too.

"When we buy lists we always ask for 'Responder' lists, even though they cost more," says Connelly. "These are lists of people who've responded to solicitations for service or merchandise that indicate an interest in the kind of lifestyle characteristic of people who buy our product. That might include snowmobile equipment catalogs, hunting supplies catalogs, magazines serving various outdoor sports—that sort of thing.

"There are two other kinds of lists—subscription and membership. Subscription to a trade magazine read by people who work in our business is pretty good. But organization membership lists usually aren't very effective. These could be people who haven't done anything in years but pay their membership dues."

"How about lists of prospects in this town and in nearby towns?" asks St. James. "Couldn't we just use a list of members of the Legion, or of the Homemakers Club?"

"Great idea," said Connelly, smiling. "But make sure that you target your mailings. A direct-mail program to the Young Republicans or to a photographers club probably wouldn't do us much good. For the jobs open now, we want to target people who are likely to have mechanical skills and experience, and women who know marketing, finance, and computers. We can't seem to get women to apply for the mechanical jobs."

"But," says St. James, "maybe you're targeting when you mail to local groups that contain a cross section of skills and interests—like, maybe, church and school directories, and the Legion's membership list."

"Oh sure," says Connelly. "I'm not putting down local membership lists. Sometimes they're fine just because they're local; people don't have to drive very far to work, and they don't have to move. I remember hearing about a retail business that used a nursery school phone directory to reach women who want to return to work part-time."

"How about our customer newsletter?" asked St. James. "That goes to a good-sized mailing list. What if we just drop a 'want ad' in there when we need employees? There's a list that already exists."

"Bingo, Johnny!" says Connelly, snapping her fingers. A second passes and she says, "My only thought about that is that we'd want to be careful about crossing vendor lines and alienating any of our customers. We don't want to appear to be pirating their employees.

"There's one other list source I want to mention." says Connelly. "Remember the company that sells educational audio and video cassettes? Well, Career Track Seminars and Publications, a company that sells and conducts training programs, would be a good source for lists of people who took training in subjects that our employees need to be familiar with. For instance, if we're looking for a supervisor, we could do a direct-mail solicitation to women who attended a Career Track supervisory management program. We could even put on our own seminar and, at the end of it, pitch our company as a place to work.

"The whole idea is to focus on people most likely to be interested, rather than just broadcasting to the whole state. It's the difference between mailing to subscribers of *Modern Machine Shop*, and running an ad in the classified section of the newspaper. You might pay more for a focused ad in the trade magazine, but results will far more than justify the expense."

Six weeks later, Johnny St. James was looking for a sales manager. In his hand he held a postcard returned from a mailer that had been sent to a list of people who bought a sales training cassette. He picked up the phone and dialed the number on the postcard.

A voice answered on the other end: "This is LeRoy Spurrier."

B̲uy lists of people in demographic groups who have a high likelihood of being qualified for your jobs. Mail them a flyer with a tear-off, postpaid card that they can return requesting more information.

P̲ractice "intrusive recruiting." Reach people who want a different job before they actually begin applying.

F̲ocus on people most likely to be interested in your jobs, rather than just broadcasting your pitch to an entire population.

CHAPTER 18

AN OUNCE OF RETENTION IS WORTH A POUND OF RECRUITMENT

When an organization regularly invests 50 percent of annual average payroll in turnover-eliminating activities, the investment is earned back in one year, according to Leonard A. Schlesinger and James L. Heskett of Harvard Business School.

If you have a problem staying fully staffed, the reason for your problem could be very simple: Too many employees leave too soon after you hire them. The solution to this problem clearly is to lengthen the duration of employment. Increase retention rate. Get employees to *stay* longer. There are two ways to do this: (1) Increase retention, and (2) Accelerate pace of recruitment. An ounce of prevention (retention) is worth a pound of cure. In other words, recruiting, hiring, and training cost a lot more than improving employee job satisfaction.

Burger King found its cost of replacing a trained hourly employee to be $1,100. The total cost of prospecting, interviewing, testing, and hiring typically amounts to 50 percent of a company's cost of doing business.

Many business people know the importance of retention, yet they still act as if the solution to an ongoing staffing problem is to run faster and faster in pursuit of new employees. Even worse, when they see their retention rate steadily and ominously dropping, they cut back on selection, training, or commitment-building activities.

"Why invest in people who aren't going to stay with us?" they reason. "There are plenty of bodies available to fill these jobs." This turns out to be one of those classic self-fulfilling prophecies: Often it is because employees aren't trained, motivated, and energized that employees leave.

Consider this scene: A recent high school graduate, Nancy, is standing behind a checkout counter in a Midwest retail store, waving a bar-code reader over merchandise. Her work day lasts eight hours; she's got another six hours left today.

As Nancy works, she yawns occasionally and shifts her weight from one foot to the other. A housewife picks up her shopping bag and passes through Nancy's station. "Have a nice day," says Nancy . . . in a monotone that would put a baby to sleep. She glances up at the clock on the wall—time is droning on.

If we watched her longer, we would notice that the only time she communicates with her supervisor is when the supervisor checks her time card or changes her schedule for the next week.

No one should be surprised when retail robots like Nancy give their notice. After enough boredom and disgust they believe that *any* job has got to be better. Employers let them go without protest. It's easy to replace them with other robots. There's really nothing that can be done to stop the exodus, they believe. They hire people who are willing, at least temporarily, to work for wages that put them below the poverty level.

The full extent of an employer's effort to develop job satisfaction or loyalty is usually no more than an offhand remark as a new employee is deposited at her or his post: "We hope you like it here." How creative.

Contrast that typical attitude with the approach taken by North American Tool and Die Company (NATD) in San Leandro, California. Thomas H. Melohn, president, CEO and part owner, says that relations with his employees are based upon the premise that employees care deeply about their work. "If you tap a well of interest and mesh it with the goals of your corporation, the results will truly stun you," he says.

NATD managers talk with employees. At least two or three times a week, they walk through the plant chatting with each worker and complimenting those who've done good work. They talk to them about future compensation, about career paths, about their contributions to the company, and what they can do to grow, personally.

Explains Melohn: "To keep people involved and caring, we work at giving real compliments—not just a perfunctory 'Good job, Smith,' but statements of sincere appreciation for each person's efforts and accomplishments. At NATD we care about our people—not just as employees, but as human beings and as friends. We try to help them in any way we can."

Melohn offers these examples of NATD's policy in this area:

- An outstanding Korean employee suffered a sudden weight loss, and was having difficulty communicating this problem to his American doctor. NATD searched the entire San Francisco metro area to find a Korean-speaking physician.
- NATD lends its employees company trucks on weekends for moving, at no charge.
- Any employee can borrow one week's pay, with no interest, for an emergency.
- The company sends flowers to every hospitalized employee or spouse.
- Each employee that gets married receives a check from the company as a wedding present.
- The owners buy doughnuts for the entire plant to celebrate paydays at the end of each month. They also distribute free season tickets to National Football League games.

Melohn summarizes: "It's much more fun to work in a happy shop."

The bonus that NATD's owners earn for treating employees like human beings and friends is *high retention rate*. There's virtually no real turnover at NATD. Productivity increased when NATD humanized its management. Here is proof that people who are satisfied in their jobs work faster and better.

Reduced turnover saves the cost of hiring and training. After launching its own employee satisfaction program, the Marriott Corporation reduced its rate of labor turnover by ten percentage points, yielding a savings significantly greater than total current profit.

You don't need a lot of money to buy employee loyalty. Many employees today will work hard, willingly, for a job they enjoy even if their pay and benefits are just average. Enjoying their work is very important to people today. Also, the opportunity to learn and grow on the job is more important to workers than it used to be.

Today's employees hate being told not to think. They hate being told to "wait for instructions," and to do nothing until someone tells them what to do. Treating people as human beings instead of as robots puts them in a mood to do their best work and to forget about leaving for a "better" job.

The autocratic boss is a thing of the past. Modern managers manage the "what," not the "how." Today, leadership has mutated from "Do it this way" to "What do *you* think?"—from leadership-by-decree to leadership-of-teams.

We hear a lot about empowerment, about teamwork, and about increasing work quality by enabling employees to do work that they enjoy. Employees want a say in how the workplace is run and how they do their jobs.

Try discarding some of your company's "trappings of hierarchy." Encourage creativity and respect for ideas. Trust employees to make the right decisions when they've been trained to do so. Give your employees the authority to make customer satisfaction decisions. They shouldn't have to consult a superior to get permission to be fair.

Help employees improve themselves with tuition grants and aid. Make recognition and rewards a company strength. Contrary to popular belief, a reward doesn't always have to be monetary. Weekend getaways at company expense, or a reserved parking space, are imaginative ways of saying, "Well done!"

Keep your employees well-informed; take them into your confidence with regard to business decisions. As James Poissant, Manager of Business Seminars at Walt Disney World once said, "In any business that depends on a frontline of employees, management must not only support it, but trust and respect it as well."

More business should do away with management-by-mandate, treating employees like mannequins without the power to think or to feel. Employees treated this way become resentful and apathetic. They eventually look for a chance to jump ship.

Some large companies invite employees to evaluate their bosses. That would be impractical in a small operation, but the principle is good. Bosses should be leaders, and leaders should get their right to lead from the consent of the led.

Bosses don't have to demand obedience when they relate with employees the same way they relate with members of their families. They'll get cooperation and accountability from employees willingly. And these employees will enjoy their jobs and never get around to looking for different ones.

Employee enthusiasm is important to nurture. People get very enthusiastic when they feel that their qualifications are improving on the job and they are headed toward promotion. They're inspired to perform at their highest levels. Naturally, productivity increases.

But when employees are exploited, and they feel that they are victims of thoughtless employers who force them to settle for "jobs" without hope of advancement, then you're creating conditions for rapid turnover.

Another effective way to win employee satisfaction is to give them the resources they need to do it. It is very discouraging to an employee to want to do a good job but to be handicapped by lack of tools.

Training employees how to achieve customer satisfaction (customer service training) is also important. Smiling is rarely enough. And it's no fun for employees to endure a steady diet of angry customers who seem to hate them and who sometimes splutter and turn purple. Every employee has a limit to his or her tolerance for such treatment. Beyond the limit of tolerance they just quit impulsively. Teach your employees how to handle irate customers.

Isn't it interesting that some business people seem to think that money spent on training is wasted in today's staffing climate? They feel that employees who've been expensively trained often leave and take their know-how to a competitor. The truth is that, in many cases, employees quit because they aren't trained to handle difficult customer situations.

Smaller businesses actually have an advantage over billion-dollar corporations because they can provide job satisfaction more easily than the big companies. No amount of money is enough to produce the genuine job commitment that personal satisfaction generates. Often, giving employees a chance to achieve their potentials and a chance for personal growth is enough. People want important work that makes a difference.

As Akio Morita, co-founder and chairman of Sony Corporation, said, "You encourage (employees) best not by offering more money, but by offering more meaning."

Bill Hewlett, one of the two people who founded Hewlett-Packard Company in a home garage, put it this way: "People want to do a good job, so just give them the tools, the opportunity, and stand back."

Make sure that employees know exactly how to do their work, then give them the tools they need to do it, tell them exactly what you expect of them, and reward them for doing their work exceptionally well. That, my friends, leads to job satisfaction which, in turn, generates the solution to staffing problems.

Retention by improving job satisfaction is much less expensive than recruiting, hiring and training.

Employees leave because they aren't trained and because employers don't motivate and energize them.

At least two or three times a week walk through the store or the plant to chat with employees and compliment those who've done good work.

CHAPTER 19

RETENTION TIP: HIRE THE ALREADY MOTIVATED

The physically challenged, the elderly, and people who were once on welfare are unlikely to spend their lunch hours and sick days looking for different jobs.

Helen Conyers, who runs the book billing department of Plenum Publishing Company, a small New York book publisher, says: "I no longer hire college graduates. I prefer welfare recipients. They are eager to learn. They come in at 8:30 a.m., even though our day starts at 9:00."

Conyers' attitude is typical of employers who subscribe to America Works, a private, profit-making company in New York City that trains and places people on welfare.

America Works trains their people in business procedures and deportment, then places them in entry-level, private sector jobs, such as office work, food service, and selling.

America Works doesn't operate outside New York City . . . yet. That means that the field is open for you in your area, should you want to start your own personnel service for welfare recipients and others in similar situations.

Meanwhile, you can work with the county welfare department to reach welfare recipients. You might be amazed at their enthusiasm. And you might be surprised to find that they are just as intelligent as people who are *not* on welfare.

Think about also asking the welfare department to put you in touch with recent immigrants, many of whom are dynamos of enthusiasm.

Hire the disabled and the elderly, too. It's in their interest to remain in a job because the difficulty of finding a job generally is greater for them than it is for unhindered adults. Give them work with a purpose, work from which they derive satisfaction, fulfilling work that offers opportunity for growth. Give them pleasant working conditions. Support them emotionally, and with the tools to do their jobs. Treat them like a member of your "family," as Wal-Mart does. Wal-Mart has more than 640,000 employees who are referred to as "associates" rather than "the staff" or "the crew." The culture in Wal-Mart stores resembles nothing so much as it does a large extended family.

Incentive programs reward employees for exceptional work. The company maintains a family spirit of cooperation through regular employee gatherings and closed-circuit telecasts to each store transmitting pep talks from managers.

Employee morale is high at Wal-Mart. People like working there, and their positive attitudes are obvious to customers. As a result, they are effective representatives of the company.

"How may I help you?" and "It was a pleasure to help you find what you want" are the kinds of conversation heard routinely at Wal-Mart stores.

Employees are enthusiastic about their work even though many are paid only marginally above minimum wage.

Wal-Mart is the most admired retail store chain in America, according to one report. Among its admirers are its employees.

Forty-three million Americans are classified as disabled by private and public agencies, according to a Congressional committee. Two-thirds of disabled adult men and an even greater percentage of disabled adult women are unemployed. The disabled population may be a gold mine of good employees, especially for firms frustrated by low skill levels and poor work attitudes of available job seekers.

With the assistance of my local Good Will Industries agency, I employ handicapped workers who assemble audiocassette packages for our training division and who work during most peak periods. I can always count on the work being done accurately and dependably. In fact, handicapped workers often exceed performance standards. They're eager to prove that they are capable and worthy of the trust we've shown in them.

You can contact handicapped workers through many nonprofit agencies throughout the United States that train the disabled and provide free job-placement service.

The Young Adult Institute in New York City does notable work. It sends disabled workers to the job along with coaches, who help provide additional training, when it's needed. Joel M. Levy, executive director of the Young Adult Institute, says that using groups such as his reduces the cost of recruitment. Clearly, many companies are well aware of this: The Prudential Insurance Company employs the deaf in its computer operations; Pizza Hut Inc. has employed some 16,000 disabled people during the past six years in restaurants located in forty-four states; Marriott and Radisson Hotels use both physically and mentally handicapped workers.

New and affordable technology makes the workplace far more accessible to the handicapped than ever before, helping to turn that segment of society into a new, valuable pool of potential employees. For example, now that computer data can be encoded into speech or Braille, blind people are employed effectively as computer programmers, telephone operators, customer service reps, and staff writers, to name but a few occupations open to them.

Unfortunately, misconceptions continue to deter employers from even considering the handicapped. One commonly held belief is that the cost of remodeling and adding facilities to accommodate the handicapped is very high. That's not true. The U.S. Labor Department asked 367 federal contractors to estimate the cost of specified physical accommodations for the disabled. 70 percent of accommodations on the Labor Department's list cost less than $100 each to construct.

Another fact that ought to break down barriers to hiring the handicapped is financial aid available from state and local agencies. Many state vocational rehabilitation departments loan adaptive devices to disabled people. Many also help to supervise and train more severely disabled workers, as well as provide job coaches.

If you want to hire disabled people, use the phrase "we hire the physically challenged" in your employment advertising. You may also:

- Contact the local county extension service and Chamber of Commerce for names, addresses and phone numbers of agencies and services devoted to the handicapped.
- Become a friend to the handicapped. Volunteer at local events such as the Special Olympics.
- Contact national associations for the handicapped and ask them to refer you to qualified handicapped people in your community.

Among these national associations are the American Council of the Blind (202-833-1251); Association for Retarded Citizens (817-640-0204); National Association for the Deaf-Blind (206-747-2611); the Epilepsy Foundation of America (301-459-3700); and the National Amputation Foundation (212-767-8400).

Remember that business people who hire the disabled not only gain quality workers, but they also receive a federal tax benefit.

No matter what the personal needs and personalities of your workers are, though, one factor is vital to retention: Job satisfaction. Some employers seem to disagree with this concept. They believe that wages and salaries should be enough. I reject the belief that work is incompatible with pleasure and satisfaction.

Work does not need to be tedious to be worthwhile. On the contrary, it can be satisfying, fulfilling, and *fun*.

When it is, employees are more productive, their work quality improves, and their loyalty increases.

Sony's Morita concurs: "Though monetary compensation is important for all of us to survive, it cannot be the only reason for working."

You, too, can create a work environment where employees want to stay. Take these steps:

- Humanize the work place.
- Train employees.
- Stress good customer service.
- Develop a pleasant, motivational work culture and environment.
- Hire people pre-motivated to work hard and to think positively about their job.
- Create upward mobility.

If you're one of those people who leaves no stone unturned, who squeezes the last drop of juice from an orange, you'll want to know about a relatively new discipline called "workplace effectiveness," which is being applied in offices throughout the country to improve employee retention.

The objective of workplace effectiveness is called Positive Effect. This occurs when an individual undergoes "an environmentally induced positive mood shift." This can be achieved in several ways.

Start with aromas. A combination of rosemary and lemon aromas is said to improve concentration, for instance. A blend of chamomile and lavender promotes relaxation. Mint odors are physically and mentally stimulating.

You might even want to give each of your employees a magnetic seat cushion. These cushions "neutralize the imbalances in the body and keep [you] energized all day," according to one cushion user quoted in the September, 1991, issue of *Success* magazine.

HIRE THE RETIRED

A recent Commonwealth Fund survey of men and women, ages fifty and older, found that nearly 70 percent of retired workers would have preferred to continue working. Another study showed that 50 percent of men leave the workforce by age sixty-two and 80 percent of them retire by sixty-nine. (The study didn't include women.)

To induce more retirees to take jobs, government needs to change its policies. Current Social Security rules should be changed. They create strong *dis*incentives to continue working after age sixty-five, notes the Committee for Economic and Policy Development in its report, "An America That Works." That's because there's a limit on the amount that retired persons can earn before they lose Social Security benefits. In 1996, that limit was $11,520 for retired persons age 65 through 69.

Here are some things you can do to induce your older workers to continue working:

- Restructure the pension plan so that it doesn't penalize workers for staying on the job past retirement age.

- Develop a flexible benefit plan that allows older workers to "buy" additional weeks of vacation, or to switch to reduced hours.

What's the advantage of using retirees? "You get workers with proven skills and a known work ethic," says Helen Axel, senior research fellow at the Conference Board in New York. Executives interviewed by Ms. Axel at twenty-eight companies said that they like retired workers because they are "highly motivated, loyal, dependable, and trustworthy. The strong work ethic and personal attributes of retirees often are the same qualities that employers say younger workers lack," says Ms. Axel.

The Travelers Companies of Hartford, Connecticut, found that retirees are more likely to report to work in bad weather than are other employees. Also, retirees have more control over their time than temporary workers, such as college students and working mothers.

Even when the skills of older and younger employees are essentially identical, executives report that attitudes toward work, and loyalty to the organization, distinguish both older workers and retirees from younger workers. "Loyalty" often translates into longevity on the job.

To find older workers, include the phrase "We hire the retired" in your advertising. Write a letter to local chapters of the American Association of Retired Persons and SCORE (Senior Corps of Retired Executives) to tell them that you are eager to hire older people. Post notices on the bulletin boards in senior centers.

After you hire a retiree, a disabled person, or a welfare recipient, tell them what is expected of them and make certain that they know how to do the work. One of the main reasons that people don't stay on the job is that they've never been told the logic and the function of their jobs.

One of the best ways to make sure that new employees are prepared is to videotape three or four experienced employees explaining how the jobs are performed.

Businesspeople who hire the physically challenged not only gain quality workers, but they also receive a federal tax benefit.

One of the best ways to make sure that new employees are prepared is to videotape three or four experienced employees talking about how to perform the jobs.

Welfare recipients generally constitute a pool of eager employees.

Chapter 20

Retaining Through Training

Every year I hear the legitimate boasts and bleats of hundreds of managers and executives throughout the nation. I learn a great deal from them about training employees to *retrain* employees. What I've learned is best conveyed through the words of the very competent people that I've had the good fortune to meet.

Richard Crawford, author of the book, *In the Era of Human Capital,* estimates the cost of replacing a worker to be one-and-a-half times the person's annual salary, considering recruiting, accounting and training costs. So if you lose a $30,000 supervisor after a year, you might as well have paid the person $45,000. That's one reason why it's a good idea to work hard to keep a good manager once you have worked hard to find one.

In this upwardly mobile society, people derive their sense of self-worth from their promotions and positions. They know that they are judged by their upward mobility. So, to retain good people, it makes sense to develop a concept of upward mobility within our organizations, and to tell every employee about promotion opportunities . . . more than once.

Training is an essential part of the upward mobility concept. It implies readiness for promotion and, therefore, opportunity. I clearly remember what one president of a packing-box manufacturing company told me as we started a tour of his plant.

"The problem with America's business institutions," he said, "is that the only way to move up is to become a manager. But we believe that an employee can grow within his or her job. They don't have to leave the job to move up. Employees know that this is our belief."

He explained that employees can grow through recognition such as tangible rewards (a week in the Adirondack Mountains in upstate New York), making them a member of the team (someone whose ideas are accepted and applied), and status improvement (give them a more impressive title).

"The most effective means we've found to convey a sense of upward mobility," said the president, "is personal growth through formal and informal training. One very effective tactic is to let employees help their supervisors with some of their tasks. Or a supervisor can assign challenging special projects. They can take an interest in their employees' personal goals as a way to give them the feeling that their chances of moving up are improving."

The company president pointed out that many firms are saving money by "de-skilling" their workforces, using more and more technology to save high labor costs.

"Technology is fine," he said, "but you've still got to give your employees a chance for personal growth or you will be accentuating your turnover problem.

"You can't doom Americans to a slow but certain impoverishment and still expect them to do quality work," he added. "Our only hope for successfully competing in the global economy is to create high-performance organizations that operate with well-educated, highly trained, and well-paid workers."

More than half the jobs created during the 1980s paid less than $12,000 per year, the poverty level for a family of four. The National Center on Education and the Economy found that most U.S. companies are seeking ways to reduce wages instead of looking for ways to "skill-up" jobs. That's an effective formula if a company intends to accelerate its turnover rate.

Paul J. Giddens, manager of Human Resources Planning at the General Electric Aircraft Engines plant in Evendale, Ohio, told me about empowerment of employees and the beneficial effect that it has upon turnover by raising self-esteem. He used the example of an illiterate paper-machine operator who doesn't have a high school diploma. "No matter how meager his skills are," said Giddens, "he still has to know what gets in the way and what keeps him from screwing up. Then, as part of a work group, he can provide good input in problem situations. Even that limited empowerment may bring the worker greater self-esteem and the motivation to further his training and education. At least the machine operator will delay any thoughts about looking for a 'better' job."

If you can keep a new employee interested in her or his job for three years, your chance of retaining that employee greatly improves. Research has shown that, after three years on the job, "longevity" sets in.

Another strategy that strengthens employee interest in their jobs (without promotion to a higher grade) is recognition among one's peers. This can be achieved in a number of ways: Call new employees "associates" after an intern period. Promote them to "junior associate" status when certain criteria are met. Later, promote them to "senior associate." Display pictures of all junior and senior associates on the wall in a high-traffic area.

The operations manager of a quality low-margin chain uses a very effective prequalifying hiring strategy that results in a capable and motivated staff. This lady, who started as an assistant buyer, told me that part of her hiring philosophy is to make it difficult for someone to land a job with her company.

"The harder it is to join up, the greater the value of the job will be in the mind of the new employee," said Celia DuCharme. "The first step in hiring is to identify a person that you want to hire. But don't tell them that you've chosen them. Wait for them to call you and ask what you've decided. Then tell them. That's the way to build the perceived value of a job. Then talk to them about performance standards for the position. Ask the applicant if he or she would be willing to spend the next several evenings watching videos that show the job being performed. Later, meet with the applicant and have him or her explain what was learned from the videos.

"We're accomplishing two things this way: First, they are being trained for the job, in a subtle way. Second, if they lack the drive or the self-confidence to do the job, you won't hear from them again. You save a lot of time if that person really can't handle the job. You save the time that the person would have spent on the job before his or her early departure from the company. You've spent about $500 on a video, but saved an estimated $1,500 in hiring expenses."

DuCharme suggested another strategy. "We believe in training before recruiting, as much as possible," she said. "One way we do that is through our learning system called 'Keeping the Customer Number One.' We provide that system to trade schools and community colleges who, in turn, build educational courses around it. We recruit out of those classes. The rationale is that a pretrained person is more likely to succeed on the job. When they succeed, they are less likely to leave for another job."

Trained or not, everyone should be hired as an "intern," I believe. Every new employee should be on probation until they finish internship.

Paul Bumbarger and Amelia Nordstrom are the president and the human resources vice president, respectively, of a company that manufactures IBM-compatible computer peripherals. They told me about their firm's thirteen-week and twenty-six-week internship programs.

"These are formula learning processes that require progressive learning until a new hire becomes a full-fledged employee," said Nordstrom. "At the end of each week, a person is evaluated on skill-development level for one or two responsibilities during the previous week or two. These periods are called modules. Someone, usually the supervisor, determines whether the person learned what was supposed to be learned. If they come up short, they repeat the learning module. Or the following week's lesson is anchored to the learning difficulties experienced during the previous module.

"What we do," Nordstrom explained, "is to break a job down into functional systems and teach those systems over time. There are books to read and cassettes to study. In thirteen or twenty-six weeks, we move a person to an associate level. In some businesses, people don't reach that level for a year or more. This internship program achieves high productivity and quality quickly. It creates a feeling of professional movement for employees. That's almost the equivalent of earning a fancier job title."

Nordstrom told me that at the end of thirty-six months of internship and work experience, a new employee has the opportunity to become a senior associate. "We make it formal when an intern becomes an associate, junior associate, then senior associate," she said. "We put their pictures on the wall. This signifies that they have *earned* the right to be on the team. By the way, it's rare for an intern graduate to quit for a better job."

Beware of providing too much "hard-fact training" at the expense of "soft-fact training." Hard-fact training is how-to-do-it instruction. Soft-fact training is "people" training—how to get along with people.

I believe that good relationships with one's co-workers are essential to quality work and good productivity. Real learning occurs when it satisfies the strongest personal need of the moment. That often turns out to be a personal relationships need.

If a twenty-six-year-old salesman is not getting along with his shipping supervisor, he's not going to learn much or work well until the two of them have patched things up. So, as often as you can, make sure that your "people situations" are taken care of before you skill-train employees. Create a compatible work team before all else.

The learning principle at work here is "anchoring" the learning. Relate subject matter to the degree of discomfort. Make employees uncomfortable about the state of their knowledge about tax laws, or how to handle irate customers or the skills they need in order to do their jobs well. Then show them salvation—a way to relieve this discomfort—through learning.

The idea, of course, is that when they have the knowledge that they need they feel more competent and they enjoy their work. Therefore, they are unlikely to look for a different job.

Far too little training time and training dollars are spent on developing compatible work relationships. Let's say that a meat packer hires me to teach soft-fact systems. What do I do? I find out where the abrasiveness and the conflicts are within that company. They may have employees who can tell me exactly how to make a hot dog, how to price it, how to order it, and how to get it on the shelf. But there's a grocer out there who is upset, and the meat packer has no idea what to say or do to make him happy.

If you train employees to maintain good relationships with the people they work with, as well as with customers and suppliers, they are unlikely to drop out and join your competitor. Teaching them how to do their work also enhances retention. But more importantly, it puts them in a mood to learn by teaching them how to become valued members of the team.

I agree with Tom Peters, the well-known consultant who wrote *Thriving on Chaos* and *Passion for Excellence*. He said: "Train, train, train until you die!"

Real learning occurs when it satisfies the strongest personal need of the moment. That often turns out to be a personal relationships need.

Create a compatible work team before you skill-train employees. Always make sure that your "people situations" are taken care of.

Personal growth through formal and informal training is one of the most effective means of conveying a sense of upward mobility.

Chapter 21

Employment Screening for Your Company

Charlie's office is in the corner of his big, old warehouse. You'd think you were walking onto a set for the play, "Death of a Salesman": leather-covered, overstuffed chairs; framed Norman Rockwell prints hanging on the walls; threadbare carpet; Charlie's desk—one of those oak jobs that weighs about five hundred pounds. It's quiet in Charlie's office, but his plant is buzzing. He manufactures custom-designed office furniture.

I visited Charlie recently, and we got to talking about business. Charlie told me that his sales manager quit after he'd been on the job for only three months. "I spent a day interviewing that guy," Charlie moaned. "I checked out his references. I paid him more money than I've ever paid a sales manager before. Still, he just left. I don't even know why."

"Maybe there was something about him you didn't know," I said. "You need to perform testing, Charlie. It helps weed out the ringers. Did you ever hire someone, and two days later think that you'd hired his brother instead? Testing can go a long way toward preventing that."

It turned out that Charlie had never given an applicant a test. Interviewing was his game. "I can tell all I need to know about people by talking to them," he insisted.

I didn't say it, but I was thinking: "Yeah, Charlie, you sure showed how good you are at interviewing when you hired that sales manager." Strange, isn't it, how people will follow a road right over the cliff?

That night, Charlie called me at home. It seems I'd gotten him thinking. "Tom, how about giving me a piece of your mind, for a price?" he asked. "I need some help with recruiting."

Before meeting again with Charlie, I gathered some research relevant to pre-employment testing and interviewing. There was one clip that I definitely wanted to show him. It was from the February 1992 issue of *INC*. magazine—an article by Ellyn E. Spragins, titled "Hiring Without the Guesswork."

She wrote: "The pickiest companies ... aim to do what might be called holistic hiring. They believe that a person's behavior, interests, and personality are crucial contributors to his or her success, or failure in a job."

More and more companies rely on pre-employment tests of personality, skills, and general ability. They realize that it is easier and less expensive in the long run to take the time to hire good employees.

I believe that even handwriting analysis has its place as a measure of personality. *Industry Week* magazine learned from a survey that more than 5,000 U.S. companies have retained handwriting analysts for personnel selection. Not very many of them publicly announce their use of graphoanalysis, though. I've read, too, that nearly 80 percent of large European companies employ handwriting analysts to help them hire. Graphoanalysts say that people project their mental processes into their writing. They subconsciously shape and organize their letters, words and lines in ways that reflect personal qualities.

I met with Charlie again at his plant. In discussing his company's hiring system, he revealed that his young human resources manager was smart and eager to learn, although he was just a business major who'd taken only one course in human relations management. He didn't know much about personnel selection, either. Charlie asked me to spend some time with the manager, and train him in some of the modern personnel selection practices.

We walked over to the human resource office and held a session with the manager, Alvin. I told him about a study in the *Psychological Bulletin* which found that traditional hiring methods—such as relying on interviews, experience, academic achievements, and education—are accurate in predicting employee success in fewer than 20 percent of the cases. The article was a pitch for pre-interview testing.

"You know that I don't trust testing," said Charlie.

"Some people don't like personality testing," I said. "They think that, in America, people should be hired if they can do the job whether or not they have a personality that's acceptable to their employer.

"I agree with most human resources people who believe that results of a personality test equip managers to assign people to jobs they enjoy. And job satisfaction is good for the company. A satisfied employee is more productive and more capable of quality work.

"If you want a good argument for personality testing," I said, "just think about the people you know who obviously are in the wrong job and who hate it. There was a supervisor who couldn't stand detail or repetitive tasks, yet performed the sophisticated inventory of 50,000 parts. Do you think he was likely to be a happy man? No sane manager would have put him in that job in the first place if he or she had known his nature.

"Most companies qualify applicants by giving them skill and general-ability tests before giving the personality test. You don't have to know if a person will feel good about doing a job until you find out whether he or she is *able* to do the job."

"Can you tell me how to use these tests and where to get them?" asked Alvin.

I reached down for my flip chart, set it on the table and turned the cover sheet. The first page was titled "Skill Tests."

Beneath the heading were the sub-titles, "Job-Related Skills" and "Negative Screening."

"Some people call skill tests 'proficiency tests,'" I explained. "Their purpose is simply to determine whether an applicant has the skills to do the job. These tests rule out applicants who don't meet a minimum standard."

I flipped to the next page, titled "General Ability Tests."

"Alvin, general-ability tests measure intelligence and technical knowledge. They can be used in a variety of ways but are used most often to measure knowledge and experience. Cognitive-ability tests are one type of general-ability test. They predict successful overall job performance rather than success at one particular task. This is especially valuable when used in a series with personality trait tests and skill tests. An applicant who can't pass a cognitive ability test probably should be considered unsuitable for a job, even if he or she scores well.

The next sheet in the flip chart was titled "Personality Tests." "These evaluate traits and personal characteristics that relate to measurable aspects of job performance, such as leadership and aggressiveness. Many companies use them to reduce turnover by evaluating applicants for the personality traits demonstrated by long-term employees."

I told Alvin that personality tests can be obtained by such companies as Profiles International (the most widely used), Minnesota Multiphasic Personality Inventory, Jackson Personality Inventory, Predictive Index, California Personality Inventory, Meyers Briggs Type Indicator, and Kolbe Connotative Index. Cost ranges from $50 to $250.

"About 20 percent of U.S. firms use personality surveys that predict on-the-job behavior and determine how a person might fit in a company," I said. "If you're interested in work attitudes, Stanton Corporation, a psychological testing and evaluation company, has a personnel selection inventory that provides a snapshot of an applicant's work attitudes. It evaluates reactions to supervision, orientation toward customer service, and attitudes toward work values, safety, and drugs."

I told Alvin that the test can be analyzed instantly on an IBM-compatible computer or scored remotely by phone. "Tests that measure characteristics similar to those rated by Stanton are marketed by London House. The Employment Inventory is similar to the London House 'Personnel Election Survey' and the Stanton inventory, except that it also predicts longevity on the job and degree of conformity with management instructions. That one costs $13.

"No matter how valid a standard, off-the-shelf test is," I continued, "you almost certainly will get a more accurate evaluation of an applicant's qualifications if you develop your own screening device. The accuracy and effectiveness of a test varies with demographics and local attitudes. You need to analyze the job you want to fill. Break it down into major components. List the skills, attributes and behaviors you're looking for. Then use the analysis as guidance for customizing a test for *your* job and as a checklist during interviews.

"With a little work you can customize your own evaluation instrument. A vendor or an expert from a local college or university can also do it for you. In customizing, look for evidence of the desired traits in a person's earlier behavior. Or you could set up scenarios for preemployment interviewing and ask candidates how they would respond in various common situations that occur in the job you're filling.

"Another option is to have a vendor conduct a local validation study for a test developed earlier. After a study, the test can be calibrated for your specific job. This approach is less expensive than developing a customized test, and it may achieve the same results. A validation study is valuable because a test is best when it's used in a company in which job requirements and the applicant pool closely resemble circumstances under which the test was created."

I also discussed with Charlie and Alvin the subject of assessing technical skills. "Testing is one option," I told them. "A company may also ask a candidate to self-evaluate his or her strengths and weaknesses. Or the candidate can be asked for recent performance reviews.

"The same person always interviews all candidates," I noted. "That way, each person will be judged by the same standards. If you have more than one interviewer, each person should rate the candidates. Pool ratings for each applicant and try to reach a consensus.

"An effective interviewer listens 80 percent of the time and takes notes. You've got to spend time evaluating a candidate's technical and interpersonal skills or you won't have enough information on which to base a hiring decision. When they do too much talking, managers frequently fall into the trap of relying on impressions rather than real feedback from the candidate.

"Obviously, every candidate is doing a selling job on the interviewer, so *never* accept what a candidate says at face value. Ask for specific, even quantifiable, accomplishments that support a candidate's claims. For example, if a candidate says that he or she significantly increased company profits, ask for figures, ask how the increase was accomplished, and ask whether the tactics employed were the candidate's own idea or were suggested by a superior or peer.

"Another way to get a reading on a person's skill level is to ask for a self-rating on a ten-point scale. A candidate who's weak in an area and wants to hide the weakness often gives an average "seven" rating. A very strong candidate is more likely to give an eight or a nine.

"Checking references may be difficult. One survey found that more than 40 percent of companies in the United States refuse to give references. One way to get people to evaluate the candidate you're considering is to ask: 'If you were counseling this person on areas of improvement in order to advance his or her career, what would you advise?' The answer you get will reveal the candidate's weaknesses. Asking how an applicant might improve isn't as intimidating to a former employer as asking, 'Did you fire this applicant?'"

I told Charlie and Alvin that the hiring "sequence" is significant. "You don't do the interview first," I insisted. "Do the skills and personality testing first. A supervisor's time is too valuable to waste on interviewing and reference checking if a potential employee doesn't make the grade on the tests. Without those tests, your hiring decision will be based upon the strength of a handshake, a nice smile, and whether or not the person is fluent and seemingly intelligent."

Nearly a year later, Charlie recalled our session. "Remember that time you spent with my man, Alvin?" he asked. "You taught him well, Tom. Every person he hired this past year, except for one, is still with us. The methods you taught him must really work because we've got some genuine winners onboard, including a few who are going to be fine managers some day. Give yourself an A-plus, Tom. Your bonus will be in the mail."

More and more companies rely on preemployment tests of personality, skills, and general ability. They realize that it is easier and less expensive in the long run.

One pitch for pre-interview testing is the fact that traditional hiring methods—interviews, experience, academic achievements, and education—are accurate in predicting employee success in fewer than twenty percent of the cases.

Qualify your applicants by giving them skill and general-ability tests before giving a personality test. You don't have to know if a person will feel good about doing a job until you find out whether he or she is *able* to do the job.

INDEX

A

AARP, *see* American Association of Retired Persons
ABT Associates, 57–58
Adopt-a-School program, 75
Advertisements, *see also* recruitment
    brochures, 103–108
        content, 112–113
    corporate reputation and, 113–114
    focused, 114–116
    vs. marketing, 111–116
American Association of Retired Persons, 98, 112, 142
American Council of the Blind, 139
American Society for Personnel Administration, 96–97
America Works, 135–136
Amoco, 32–33
Aromatherapy, 140–141
Association for Retarded Citizens, 139
Autry, James, 23
Axel, Helen, 142

B

Belous, Richard, 92–93
Birch, David, 6
Block, Marilyn, 1
Bowes, Lee, 38
Breaking with Tradition, 56

Brochures, 103–108
    content, 106–107
    flyers, 120
Brown, Moore and Flint, 31
Bumbarger, Paul, 149
Burger King Corporation, 77, 82, 126
Burnout, 95
Bush, George, 27–28
Business Week, 45

C

California State University Fullerton, 75
Career Track Seminars and Publications, 122
Carlin, Roger Q., 91
Case Western University, 27
Catalyst, 56
CDM, *see* Central Demographic Model
Center for Work Force Preparation and Quality Education, 78
Center of influence, 31–32
Central Demographic Model, 10–12
Coaching, 45, *see also* education; training
Cognetics, Inc., 6
Colonel's tradition program, 99

Committee for Economic and Policy Development, 141
Commonwealth Fund, 141
Computer diskette brochure, 104
Conference Board, 142
Connelly, Esther, 119–122
Connexion, 53
Conyers, Helen, 135
CPS Employment Services Network, 88
Crawford, Richard, 145
Crew Education Assistance Program, 77
Cunningham, Russ, 94–95
Customers, employees as, 63–65

D

Death of a Salesman, 155
DECA, *see* Distributive Education Clubs of America
Deere Credit Corporation, 95–96
Deming, W. Edwards, 24–25
Dermatis, Sophie, 56, 60
Development, staff, 42–44
Dickie Dees, 13
Disabled employees, 135–141
Distributive Education Clubs of America, 104
Domino's Pizza, 25–26

DuCharme, Celia, 148–149
Dunhill Mailing Lists, 105

E

Eastman Kodak Company, 76–77
Easton, Roger, 67–72
Editorial fact sheet, 71
Education, *see also* coaching; training
   corporate programs, 76–78
   incentive programs, 82–84
   linking work to, 81–84
Electronic network recruitment, 52–53
Employees
   aromatherapy and, 140–141
   burnout, 95
   coaching, 45
   customers as, 63–65
   development, 42–44
   disabled, 135–141
   flex-time programs, 91–98
   incentive programs, 136–137
   intelligence of, 3–4
   job-changing stages, 2
   job satisfaction, 19–23
   job-sharing arrangement, 95
   managers
      hierarchy, pyramid-type, 23
      unqualified, avoiding, 2–3
   moral, 125–132
   part-time, 95–96, 107–108
   promotion opportunities, 41–48
   referral programs, 35–38
   replacing, cost, 145
   retirees as, 98–100
   retraining, 125–132, 145–152
   screening, 155–163
   training, 43–44
   women, 55–61
Employment agencies, 51–53
Employment Inventory, 160

F

Families and Work Institute, 93
Fearless workplace, 23–25
Feminine Mystique, 56
Flex-time, 91–98
Flyers, *see* brochures
FMI, *see* The Food Marketing Institute
Focused advertising, 114–116
The Food Marketing Institute, 84

Freud, Sigmund, 27
Friedan, Betty, 56
Fuchs, Jim, 9
Fuchs Copy Systems, 9
Future needs/function chart, 45–46

G

Garrison, Tom, 31–33
General Electric, 147
General Electronics Trading and Manufacturing Company, 67–72
Gibbons, Joseph, 6
Giddens, Paul J., 147
Golden Age Clubs, 112
Good Humor, 13
Good Will Industries, 112, 137
The Great American TV Poll, 28
Guinn, Stephen F., 76–77

H

Handwriting analysis, 157
Harvard Business School, 125
Herzberg, Frederick, 27
Heskett, James L., 125
Hewlett, Bill, 132
Hewlett-Packard, 132
Hofstede, Geert, 27
Hopkins, Kevin, 56–58
Hygienic factors, 27

I

INC, 156
Industry Week, 157
Infincom, 5
Intelligence, employees, 3–4
InternAmerica, 88
Interning, 81–82
Interviews
  people for, selecting, 1–2
  time factor, 15–16
In the Era of Human Capital, 4, 145

J

Jackson Personality Inventory, 159
J.C. Penny, 65
Job description, 46–48
Job fairs, 84
Job satisfaction, 19–23
Job sharing, 95
  woman and, 96–98
Jobtrak, 88

K

Kentucky Fried Chicken, 99, 113
Kodak Scholars Program, 76–77
Koether, Mike, 5
Kolbe Connotative Index, 159

L

Learning Center, 22
Learning opportunity list, 43
Lear's, 11
Levi Strauss, 97
Levy, Joel M., 138
Lifetime, 28
Lind, Jim, 32–33
Loeser, Herta, 56, 58–59
Los Angeles Times, 93

M

Macan, Theresa Hoff, 11–12
Magnetic seat cushion, 141
Mailing lists, 105
    targeting, 119–123
Male, Bruce, 47
Management Decisions, Inc., 27
Managing Work and Family, 94
Marketing, 111–116
Marriott Corporation, 129
Martin, Robert, 78
Maslow, Abraham, 26–27
McClelland, David, 26
McDonalds', 99
McIntyre, Charles, 98
Megasys Corporation, 75
Melohn, Thomas H., 15–16, 127–129
Meredith Corporation, 23
Meyers Briggs Type Indicator, 159
Michaels, Bonnie, 94
Minnesota Multiphasic Personality Inventory, 159
Modern Machine Shop, 122
Monaghan, Tom, 25–26
Morita, Akio, 132
Motivation
    expectancy in, 27
    two factor theory of, 27
Motorola Company, 78

N

The Naisbitt Group, 1
NATD, *see* North American Tool & Die Company

National Amputation Foundation, 139
National Association for the Deaf-Blind, 139
The National Center on Education and the Economy, 147
National Planning Association, 92–93
Networks, 87–88
News releases, 71
New York Telephone Company, 78
No One Need Apply, 38
Nordstrom, Amelia, 149–150
North American Tool & Die Company, 127–129

O

O'Connell, Helen, 97
Olmstead, Barney, 56, 59–60
Operation transition, 88
ORC, *see* Original Research Corporation
ORC II Merit University, 43–44
Original Research Corporation, 43–44

P

Pacific Gas and Electric, 94–95
Passion for Excellence, 152
Payne, Nicole, 97
Personality tests, 157–161
Personnel Election Survey, 160
Peters, Tom, 152
Peterson's Connexion Services, 53
Phillips, Roger, 55–57, 59, 61
Pieper, Ann, 91
Pizza Hut Inc., 138
Plenum Publishing Company, 135
Poissant, James, 130
Polaroid Corporation, 57
Popular Mechanics, 105
Positive Affect, 140
Pre-employment tests, 156–161
Print brochure, 104–105
Profiles International, 159
Promotion opportunities, 41–48
Prudential Insurance, 138
PSP: Human Resource Development, 76–77
Psychological Bulletin, 157
Public relations, 69–72
Purdum, Helen, 97

Q

Quaker Fabric Corporation, 35
Quick-Trip Corporation, 104–105

R

Recruitment
  advertising, *see* advertisements
  agencies, 51–53
  CDM, 10–12
  cost, avoiding, 125–132
  employee's role, 35–38
  flex-time and, 91–98
  future needs/function chart, 45–46
  internships and, 81–82
  interviews
    selecting, 1–2
    time factor, 15–16
  job description, 46–48
  job fairs, 84
  managers, 2–3
  mishires, cost, 4–6
  networks, 87–88
  process, importance, 1–7
  public relations and, 69–72
  routines, 31–32
  small business edge, 19–23
  targeted plan, 10–15
  time allotted to, 31–34
  training programs and, 83–84
  via schools, 75–79
  women and, 55–61
Retention, 67–69
  education incentive programs, 82–84
  rate, 125
Retirees
  hiring, 141–143
  part-time employment, 98–100
Right Way Manufacturing Company, 119–122
Riordan, Michael, 4–5
Rockwell, Norman, 155
Romano & Sanfilippo, 42, 56, 96
The Roundtable, 55–56

S

Sanfilippo, Barbara, 42, 56, 58, 96–97
Saturn Corporation, 21–22
Schervish, Herb, 82
Schlesinger, Leonard A., 125

Schools, recruitment via, 75–79
Schwartz, Felice, 56, 59–61
SCORE, *see* Senior Corps of Retired Executives
Self-actualization, 26
Senior Corps of Retired Executives, 142
Slutzky's method, 13–14
Small business, recruitment advantages, 19–23
Sony Corporation, 132
Spragins, Ellyn E., 156
Spurrier, LeRoy, 119, 122
St. James, Johnny, 120–121
Staff, *see* employees
Stein, Stanley, 64
Struthers, Mabel, 91

T

Talent scout cards, 37
Targeted recruiting plan, 10–15
Terry, Carl, 92
Thomas, Barbara L., 53
Thriving on Chaos, 152
Towers Perrin, 6
Training, 43–44, *see also* coaching; education
current employees, 145–152
disabled workers, 137–141
employees, cost, 125–132
programs, recruitment and, 83–84
Transamerica Life Companies, 100
TravCorps, 47
Travelers Insurance Companies, 99, 142
Turnover, *see* retention

U

The University National Bank and Trust Company, 36–37
University of Missouri, St. Louis, 12
U.S. Chamber of Commerce, 78
U.S. Labor Department, 138

V

Value system, 27
Video brochure, 103–104
Video production, 105–106
Vogue, 11
Vroom, Victor, 27

W

Wal-Mart, 136–137
Walt Disney World, 130
Welcome Wagon, 12
Wilson, Larry, 22, 25, 68
Winninger, Tom, 83
Winninger Institute, 83
Withers, Arlene Falk, 100
Women
    job-sharing programs and, 96–98
    recruiting, 55–61

Women in Business, 105
Workplace
    aromatherapy in, 140–141
    fearless, 23–25
    humanization of, 25–29
Wright, Stanley C., 76–77

Y

Young Adult Institute, 138

Thomas J. Winninger works within industries to create strategies that gain market advantage. He is the founding director of Winninger Institute for Market Strategy.

If you would like to know more about inviting Tom to share his strategies with your industry, receive information about his SkillTECH training programs, or request a complimentary audio cassette of one of Tom's presentations. . . .

call toll free: (800) 899-8971

or write: Winninger Institute
3300 Edinborough, Suite 701
Minneapolis, Minnesota 55435

or fax this page to: (612) 896-9784

NAME:_____

ADDRESS:_____

CITY/STATE/ZIP:_____

PHONE:_____

FAX:_____

TYPE OF PRODUCT/SERVICE?_____